clean

clean

A story of addiction, recovery and
the removal of stubborn stains

MICHELE KIRSCH

Published in 2019 by Short Books Ltd
Unit 316, ScreenWorks, 22 Highbury Grove,
London, N5 2ER

10 9 8 7 6 5 4 3 2 1

Copyright © Michele Kirsch 2019

A CIP catalogue record for this book is available
from the British Library.

ISBN: 978-1-78072-381-5

Cover design by Georgia Vaux
Cover photo © Michele Kirsch

Printed at CPI Group (UK) Ltd, Croydon, CR0 4YY

For Kitty and Rory Grew,
and for Una Davies

"*Unless everything is tidy and pleasant all about one, people cannot even begin to enjoy life. I cannot endure mess.*"

Stella Gibbons, *Cold Comfort Farm*

Chapter One

In 1967 my father was taken out by a swift blow to the head while travelling from New York to Canada. "Human error" was the legal reason given for the collision of a freight train with his commuter carriage. I saw one black-and-white photo of the accident in an old newspaper, many years later. There were two casualties: my father, and a nun. The photo showed the carriage of the long train on its side, forming an angle of about 60 degrees with the embankment. He was sleeping, we were told, and something heavy fell on his head. All I hoped was that he really was asleep, and that the nun was, too.

We were in Liverpool when the news arrived. The phone was at the bottom of the stairs in the corridor by the door. This was the customary place for the phone then: draughty, no privacy, uncomfortable. They were put in places to ensure nobody stayed on them for very long as they were so expensive. My grandfather rushed to get it and in typical understatement bellowed, "SID IS DEAD! HE'S DEAD!" And my mother at the top of the stairs melted into her nightgown, leaving a little puddle of whiteness, a ghost melting below the sheet.

There were hushed discussions about who would house or fix this broken family. One option was to stay in

Liverpool. One option was for my sister, nine, and myself, six, to go to Caracas to be looked after by my uncle and aunt, while my mother "got better". At some point she took charge and felt it was best for all of us to move back to Queens, New York, where she and my dad had started their family. The apartment was only a few miles from the airport, where he worked at BOAC.

When we got back to the flat in Queens, a lot of my father's stuff was still there: his bathrobe, his cigar holder, his smell. There was no good evidence to allow the idea that he might never come back. He was just... away. This was not a lie or euphemism trotted out by the attending adults to buy time, to eventually explain this "death" thing. It was just my six-year-old understanding of it. He was not there, corporally, but he was very much there, on some other level that was beyond any sort of cognitive logic. He just had a different shape, an invisible one. My sister and I shared one room, my mother and dead father, another. Our family ran grief like other people run marathons. To be respectably sad was to mourn for ever. This maxim proved to be a destructive lie, but at the time and, in times to come, it was my kind of normal.

Our post-father and -husband lives were filled with lawyers and doctors and well-meaning friends from the neighbourhood. Stanley, the pharmacist, used to send a boy round with a stapled bag of drugs to alleviate widowhood. My mother had consolation from her doctor, an old-fashioned, "Tell-me-about-your-childhood" type, with a fat prescription pad. The top drawer of her bedside table rattled with the comforting sound of those little orangey-brown prescription pill bottles, in the days before childproof caps. All different colours, some full, some nearly empty; some cut in half, some the size of something you would give a large, sick animal. My mother weighed about seven stone.

I had Dr Drucker – a man with the surname of a dirty limerick – and he provided me with various tonics and potions to help combat the permanent nausea of grief. I had no vocabulary for this feeling of bile rising in my throat, rejecting food, rejecting life, nor did I have the words to express a vague terror, a fear of the fear, a sense of doom, without actually knowing what doom was. Doom was just this thing that meant people you loved did not come back.

But there was someone who was reliable and always came back. This was Emma, our cleaner. She came once a week and made everything in the apartment look and smell so much better. Tall and sturdily built, she smelled of clean linen and Johnson's Baby Powder. I used to cling onto her muscular leg while she did the ironing and we listened to Top 40 radio, Cousin Brucie on WABC. We went wild when the Jackson Five came on. She'd stop ironing and lift me in her arms, and we would dance and sing along to "I Want You Back". What or who I wanted back... I could not have, but I could still have these little moments of joy, in Emma's arms, singing along with Michael. To be wild with joy, to love a pop band, crank the radio up when they came on, was the opposite of being wild with grief. To this day, when I hear the Jackson Five, I have a delicious olfactory illusion of clean, steam-iron smells, of Emma's talcy-thin sheen of sweat seeping through her housework turban, and I can almost hear her saying, "We love this one, Kangaroo..." She called me Kangaroo because I used to leap up to her middle and attach myself there, when she was ironing or hoovering. *Boing*, I would leap up and attach myself, assured of her balance, strength and agility, as she ironed and danced with my legs gripped around her middle.

Eventually, when I first moved away from home to go to university, I became a cleaner myself. I had no illusion that being a cleaner would make me big and strong and calm and joyful, like Emma, for I spent large chunks of my childhood and adolescence undersized, weak, nervous and unhappy. I didn't think a stack of ironing and a can of lemon furniture polish would undo all that. It was just a good, honest, simple job that I could fit in between classes and anxiety attacks.

I cleaned big houses in Boston, where I went to university, briefly, and promptly dropped out. I enjoyed cycling from one huge house to another. Grand houses, with elaborate winding staircases rising from marble-floored entry halls, which were as big as flats themselves. When everyone left for work or school, I would stand in the entry hall and bellow, "Honey, I'm home!" because it was something I never heard in my own home. The clean would take four or five hours, because I polished vast sets of tarnished silver, as well as doing all the usual dusting, mopping, scouring and tidying. Then I would do one thing that was a bit wrong, a bit naughty, for the thrill of possibly getting caught. Oh, I don't mean stealing anything, or eating their food, or drinking their booze, or taking their drugs. I would just do something you can only do in big houses, like slide down the bannister on a dust cloth, or surf down the last flight of stairs on a flattened cardboard grocery delivery box.

When I first worked as a cleaner, it gave me a taste of the life I thought was in store, not the job I would return to, after doing "smart" jobs. Nice big house, kids, some sort of genteel career involving my own home office, teenagers blaring music from their rooms, a crock pot sizzling away in the kitchen. When I finally had something like that life I glimpsed so many years ago, I was the one blaring music from my room, necking drugs and drink and making an almighty mess of my own home and family. Cleaning, eventually, was the only option left. I was finishing my working life as I began, in a dumb job that you do when you can't really do anything else.

Now I clean places that are interesting at first, but there is often a uniformity to them. After the third or fourth clean I just do my stuff. All my body has to do is go through certain motions, pushing, wiping, dusting, scrubbing. My mind can go anywhere. If I think hard enough I am transported somewhere else, even as my hand is fishing long strands of hair from a bath plughole.

That said, all cleans are a mixture of fleeting memories, mine and those of my clients. Every object that stirs a memory in me, no matter how small, is déjà vu for a life that isn't mine to remember. I see a conch shell; I remember my father putting one to my ear as a child and saying, "Listen. The sea is in there." I put it to my ear, then I polish it and put it back. I clean badly made things that break off in my hands. Kitchen cupboard doors come off their hinges. Blinds fall away from the windows. Frantically, I try to put them back into place, on the broken thing that was supporting them.

I clean – and this is the least satisfactory aspect of the job – flats or houses which, to the naked eye, are immaculate, and which I make look worse. Sometimes, when the sun is shining, and I am inside the murkiest of mushroom-sprouting fridges, I feel like Freddy Mercury in the "I Want to Break Free" video. Other times, I think back to when this activity was part of my non-paid job description, cleaning my own oven, my own fridge, as a wife and mother. I remember my toddlers emptying the kitchen cupboards of all my pots and pans and banging on them with spoons. I remember following a homemade Play-Doh recipe with flour, salt, water and oil and making a glorious mess, all of us covered in flour. I remember what it was like to be part of a happy, functioning, loud and messy family. What it felt like to step on an Action Man or a Lego piece barefoot at three in the morning. Holding them close: sweaty, outraged bodies wriggling, overfilled nappies creeping down chubby legs. Singing a song my grandfather used to sing to me: "I went to the races last July, far, far, away. I bet on a horse named Kidney Pie, far, far away. The horse came in, I danced with glee, I went to get my LSD, oh the bookie, where was he? Far, far away."

Chapter Two

I didn't really believe my father was actually dead until I read it in the *New York Times*. My version of things was that he was bored, and he had used his free travel with BOAC to go somewhere more interesting than Queens, but that eventually he would return to us, contrite, and he would make pancakes on Sunday, and he and I would go to the Chinese laundry, like we always did, to pick up the overstarched sheets in the brown parcel, and my mother would be overjoyed.

I was fourteen when I went to the NYC public library, the big one mid-town, with lions at the front, that appears in so many films. They had microfiche back then, sort of screen shots of every newspaper that still existed in paper form. I went down to the microfiche room and ordered a copy of the *New York Times* dated 13 August 1967, the day after his accident. I figured if it was in the paper at all it would be tiny, but there was a three-quarter page piece, with the photo of a train carriage on its side. Maybe the one my father was in. I read the whole article, still not believing it to be any part of my life, until the last paragraph mentioning the two fatalities and explaining that Sidney Kirsch, of such and such address, had died, leaving a wife and two small children.

When I got back to Queens, I felt as if I knew something for sure. I had grown up. Some people describe this as the moment when they know there is a God, or some Higher Power. At this moment in time, all I believed in was death, the power of it to destroy not only the life of the dead person but of all the people who knew and loved them. The death of a person you are close to can be the ultimate get-out clause. In my experience, no one expects you to be normal after someone you love dies. You can quietly withdraw from life or the stuff that sustains life – eating, activities, being engaged and engaging, getting on with things.

I think to some extent my mother, sister and myself played this get-out-of-life-free card for a long time, though of course my mother still had to be a mother, to two very difficult – in different ways (myself, afraid of everything, my sister, cross, very cross) – children.

A few years after my father was killed, I made a best friend, Judy. Her parents were very left-wing and went down to all the peace marches and civil rights protests in Washington. In 1972 they campaigned for the Democratic candidate George McGovern, who was going to stop the war. Judy and I stood outside the polling stations, handing out leaflets for McGovern, just in case some Republican at the last minute decided to change his or her mind.

I seemed to live at least part time in Judy's house, which was full of laughter and music and a surfeit of parents – at least two – plus visiting aunties or nanas. The mealtimes there were filled with stories, told with great animation and comical gestures – the roll of the eyeballs, the jazz hands, the exaggeration of accents or postures – and her father declaiming at various intervals, "Am I right, or am I right?" It was like watching a show. There were family in-jokes which I was let in on, being an honorary member of that family. My favourite was when everyone was bickering at the table and someone would pipe up, "Is everybody happy?" and this would break the tension. I also got to observe the sweet secrets and innocent conspiracies of a supremely happy marriage. One day Judy's mum went on a health-food kick and made bile-coloured milkshakes out of a powder called Tiger's Milk, leaving Judy, her dad and me with three tall, frosty glasses of the stuff, the three of us sitting at the table and staring at the drink with rising panic. When Judy's mum left the kitchen, her dad took a sip, shuddered, and took our glasses to the sink, quietly tipping out the contents while making a sealed-lips gesture with his hand. This was the stuff of normal family life, a wonderful place I could visit, but not somewhere I could live full time.

My own mum was chic and cosmopolitan, shunning the trappings of domestic drudgery, preferring to order take-away or stockpile frozen dinners. In later years she told me my father, too, had been cosmopolitan, preferring to go out, explore the great city, or other cities, rather than look at houses in suburbs, or put up shelving with spirit levels. They were of the same mind. Anything to do with cooking and cleaning bored her, or reminded her that dinner for four was now dinner for three, or even two, as I was impossible to feed, a slave to the eruptions and pains of my stomach. My sister, while not picky, viewed any attempt at a new dish with great suspicion, much sniffing, and the forensic removal of unidentified herbs. So my mum was relieved to find a new line of complete frozen dinners called TV dinners, which were meant to be eaten on trays in front of the telly, though we had to eat ours at the table. I liked this set-up. It was easier to refuse food that had been frozen by Swanson than a meal my mother had slaved over. My mum would survey the contents of the freezer and ask if we wanted the Salisbury steak (basically a giant burger) or turkey with all the trimmings. I quickly learned the minimal prep of these frozen dishes, tearing away bits of tin foil to brown the potatoes or crisp the small segment of apple pie. As they looked so much like the meals we had on airplanes, their preparation, I felt, would stand me in good stead to be a stewardess on BOAC, the airline my father and mother worked for, and a job I felt I was destined to do, even though I hated flying.

My sister inhabited a mysterious teenage world, learning the subtle arts of make-up application, hair-ironing, and being popular, which she was. At night, in our twin candlewick-bedspread-covered beds, I would study the curves her body made through the sheets and blankets, an S shape on its side, and hourglass when upright. Would this ever happen to me? Like most older sisters with pesky kid siblings, she kept me at a healthy distance, though music would bring us together and playing records or the radio, for the short while we liked the same kind of music, shattered the ghostly silence of the flat. The Jackson Five always reduced me to mild states of hysteria. We'd stand on our beds singing into hairbrushes, anything by the Jackson Five, the Temptation's glorious "Psychedelic Shack", Freda Payne's "Band of Gold" or "Love Child" by the Supremes – a story about a child born out of wedlock which was even worse than not having a dad through death. Stomach drugs and pop music were the only things that could really change the way I felt, providing relief and pleasure and escape. (As I got older and the stomach drugs were supplanted by sedatives and alcohol, I found I had to play the music at higher volume, to counter the narcoleptic effects of the drink and drugs.)

I could also escape to Judy's. The family were well-off, and they had a holiday home in Long Island, a place called Cutchogue. They used to invite me out there over the school holidays and I remember the first time was winter. We stopped on the way at what must have been one of the first shopping malls. In the middle of this mall was a Santa Claus, in a little grotto with Styrofoam snow, which stuck to everything. Judy said, "Let's go, let's go sit on Santa." And I said, "We can't. We're Jewish, he'll know!" Not only did I imagine Santa chucking us off his lap saying, "Jews! Be off!" but also that any presents we got during the euphemistically called "holiday season" would be taken from us and given to Christian children. I sat on Santa's lap and asked for a Malibu Barbie, complete with trailer, but I told him I understood that the Christians probably came first.

"Ho, ho, ho," he chuckled drearily. "Are those your parents over there, at the make-your-own perfume stall?"

"Yes," I lied.

"Ask them to take you to Toys R Us. It's on the second level, you may want to mention that, too. Ho, ho, ho."

My real mother, exhausted by the duel demands of two bratty children and a job she didn't want, remained for great lengths of time in her bedroom, the stale scent of chain-smoked Navy Cut cigarettes hanging heavily in the claustrophobic air. BOAC had provided her with a shift pattern job, dealing with difficult or troubled passengers – a job she was perhaps singularly unsuited for, being a soft touch and not one to toe the corporate or customs line, or relish having to confiscate smuggled mangoes and explain to tearful passengers why they had to leave agricultural products at the airport. Her friends and shrink felt work would be therapeutic. She thought it was a pain in the arse.

I think she felt life without my father was something to be endured, not enjoyed. Those of us who have not experienced this sort of suffering are quick to judge those who do not bounce back from loss, but I admire the brutal honesty of her sustained misery. I think she felt it was pointless to pretend to be content with her lot in life, to do the brave-face thing. She often said, when I was old enough to understand, that a part of her died with my father, and I could see the truth in that.

She had an aversion to atmosphere, to opening her windows. It would let the heat in, or the cold in, or perhaps air the room of a smell that might have held a trace of my father. She seemed most at peace sitting on the edge of the bed, surrounded by paperwork, bank letters, official-looking things, now and then a light-blue aerogramme from her parents. She drifted off in, I suspect, a narcotic haze some nights, as there were knock-out drugs for bereavement. It was the received wisdom at the time that what could not be endured could be medicated. As she dozed, the radio softly reported tales of horror. In those days the tranquillisers were very strong, and her grief, which was pathological and sustained, was treated as a medical matter. What could not be endured could at least be dulled or sufficiently numbed. She slept through Vietnam, assassinations, campus unrest. Slept, smoked and waited for the door to ring. It might be Stanley's drug delivery guy. It might be the grocery store delivery. It might be one of her friends, but, "What do they know?" she told me. I mean, what did they *really* know, with their houses, their husbands, their unscathed children, their Betty Crocker cake mixes? And wall ovens. It was the new thing back then, an oven built into your wall. My mother felt it was all ridiculous: domesticity, suburbia, cars. People's husbands got better jobs and they moved out to the suburbs, Long Island. We stayed in Queens, where my mum still had her memories, and memorabilia.

This may be one of the reasons I like to clean. I crave the memorabilia of others, for it tells a story I don't really know. It means little to me personally, and yet, I can create a scenario. It is not imbued with memory, with preciousness, with sentiment of my own making. Photographs, for example – framed photos of the childless in the flats and houses I clean, they tell a private story. Maybe a photo here and there of a parent or grandparent doing something of his or her time: wearing a vintage hat that the same couple would pay 60 quid for in a vintage market. Smoking cigarettes out of a cigarette-holder. Girls in old-fashioned swimming costumes linking arms on a freezing beach holiday in England. A baby in a ridiculously oversized pram. Baby sitting up, wearing a bonnet. Great-grandparents? Likely. I clean so many flats of couples who have so many pictures of themselves, clearly gazing at each other in adoration. Without exception they are young, more than averagely attractive and quite often a little bit drunk, maybe pulling faces in a hotel photo booth... And yet they are not old enough to have built up or stored that many personal memories.

Collections are another mystery. Are these collections tangible evidence of real memories, or just stuff to make the people who own them have something to talk about, to profess a passion for, with which to make better memories than the real ones? I puzzle over one who thinks it's quirky to collect Smurf-related paraphernalia, to show she is not just a business-minded web designer, but also a little bit wacky, a little bit interested in crap stuff that existed before her time. She has a lot of expensive natural-health supplements for period pains. Another one has a poster of *Withnail and I*, Withnail sitting in despair, "I" looking hapless and disconsolate. Which is how he looks for the entire movie, as I recall. The guy is in property development or oil or something lucrative that lets him work for only six months of the year and have fun for the other six. I suspect he was not even born the year *Withnail* was released, which is not to dampen or dissuade his enthusiasm for the film. I suspect, but don't know, as I deal mainly with his live-in babe girlfriend, that he has a nostalgia for a time that existed before his.

And then there is the stuff of remembrance. You just know that whoever owned this thing, these things, is dead and this thing is cherished. I remember my mother wearing my father's tartan dressing-gown. Keeping all of his book-of-the-month collection books, great multi-volume works of history by Churchill. Perhaps never read, but they looked stately. Not a shrine, not a museum, but the stuff that made him him: comfortable, educated, crazy for travel. The little figurine of the man playing the tin drum from a shop in Barbados, the flip-out folded fans with the BOAC logo. The ashtrays that had recipes for cocktails written on them. You can hold this stuff, you can dust it, but you can't put your arms around it.

When you are cleaning, you are tidying the stuff of nostalgia, the stuff people think is important, the stuff someone they love left behind or what they will leave behind to someone when they die. I think of the woman who had the novelty lamp with the light-up, moving penis. She eventually got rid of it, but I could not imagine her friends bickering over it after her demise. You could not cry and say, "I really want the penis lamp" in the same breath.

Cleaning, London 2016
THE CAREER WOMAN

THIS IS AN EASY GIG. She lives a ten-minute walk from me. Her flat is small. The only snag is the spare bedroom, where the bed is a platform job, flush to the window. In order to change the sheets, I have to clamber on the bed and imagine all the strangers that have slept there, for it is an Airbnb. She has pillows with pictures of Hindu gods on them, sometimes on her bed, sometimes on the guest bed. The shelves you can reach from the platform have art books, a carved Hindu god and a framed picture of the main characters in *Fawlty Towers*. This is an in-joke possibly beyond the understanding of many of her young visitors.

To change the guest bed, I have to be on it and position myself in such a way that I can lift a corner of the mattress to tuck in the fitted sheet. More often than not, I slip down between the small gap at the window side of the bed and find myself perched, just about, on the tiny window ledge, unable to pull myself back up, and unable to navigate a tunnel through the bespoke drawers under the bed. I once spent an hour in this ridiculous position, trying with my not-strong-enough arms to press myself back onto the platform, or push the drawers out with my foot so I could get out underneath. I wondered what it looked like to passers-by, this flattened creature, caught like a confused wasp, and spent my window-gap time in terror that the lady would return and find me, splayed, insane-looking, trying so hard to be a normal house cleaner. I wonder what it must feel like to be an independent woman who is strong, attractive, financially stable, astute, aspirational and just a good person, someone I would want to be friends with if I were not her cleaner, stuck between her window and her platform bed. Before I start the clean, I pray to the Hindu god, don't let me get stuck, don't let me get an asthma attack emptying the Hoover. Let her walk into the flat after I've done it over and think, wow, it looks so much better.

Chapter Three

The dead people I know live in my head, and offer up a chorus of approval for every decision I make, no matter how stupid that decision is. And it usually is a stupid decision: me and my dead friends think it is a good idea – no, a great idea – to get more hammered and take more drugs. They may not have approved while they were living, but now they are dead, I decide what we all think is best for me. The dead are so agreeable.

I knew none of this at six. Or even fourteen, when I went to the library. But I had an inkling that death had some tremendous power over those who had lost someone and were kind of killing time before their own time was up. This was what I observed: it is hard to be the prettiest, or the cleverest, or the funniest, but it is dead easy to be the saddest. That I could do.

Death made me nervous. It was so unpredictable. I preferred events that ran to a timetable, like TV. When I was growing up there was no concept of screen time, or of telly being bad for you, so it was wonderful to get sucked into the box, into this bright and brash and perfect world. Hours on end, glued to sitcoms and variety shows, eating Pop Tarts and drinking vanilla-flavoured Nutrament – a high-calorie drink suggested by my doctor to put flesh on my troubled, skinny bones – I found solace. Inside the box. Even the adverts promised a life beyond my wildest dreams. If you just bought stuff – Oscar Myer wieners, Charlie perfume, Doublemint chewing-gum, Diet Rite cola ("Folks not on a diet, try it") or Gee Your Hair Smells Terrific shampoo – you could be one of those happy people living in a seemingly endless musical, men falling at your feet, children (perhaps yours) munching happily on recovered-meat products... there was nothing not to love. Nobody ever died on TV either, at least not on the TV I watched. Certainly, never the adverts.

There was one advert for an antiperspirant which enchanted me. It showed various, achievably attractive women in mildly nerve-wracking situations. One woman confesses to a camera: "Nervous is meeting your boy-friend's family, all sixteen of them." Another is in a car and says with mock exasperation: "Nervous is taking your driving test, for the fourth time."

The solution was "Soft and Dri" which would stop you sweating in these hair-raising moments. There was no scenario that matched mine: nervous is when you wake up in the morning sick and just want to stay in bed all day, listening to pop radio and then swap over to TV to watch variety shows.

Could that be all it took? Dabbing this phallic roll-on under my arms instead of waiting in for the man from the drugstore? Because of a puberty that was delayed by nerve-induced malnourishment until I was nearly seventeen, I did not actually sweat. Still, I spent my pocket money on the promised Valium of roll-ons: "Soft and

Dri". It stained all my clothing but did nothing for my nerves.

The TV shows I liked best were the variety ones, with all the dancing and singing and comic sketches. I loved the Sonny and Cher show, but Cher in particular. I dreamed embryonic lesbian dreams of Cher, even before I knew what lesbians were. Cher could rescue me. Cher would come to our block of flats on her horse, dressed (just barely) in Indian garb (she had Cherokee blood, she said in one song), and I would get on the horse with her and we'd ride off onto Queens Boulevard, past the deli, the pizza place, the grocery store, the porno cinema, and everyone would go, "Look, there's Michele and Cher" – having obviously been made aware of Michele's hidden talent for horsemanship, her possible Cherokee blood and uncanny ability to sing any Top 40 song word-perfectly after one listen.

I had a notion of what sort of woman I wanted to be and look like, but it seemed such a far way off. I was always what is now called "young for her age" and looked about nine until I was sixteen, when I looked about twelve. One thing that was happening was that Judy was turning into a young woman at about the right age. She grew breasts, started periods, started to get noticed by boys. I remained a child. Straight up and down. This was not a deliberate ploy on my part. I just didn't seem to have the necessary appetite to take in the amount of nutrients to make my curves grow, my hormones start hormoning, my budding sexuality bud.

One summer we were in the city, taking the eternal

bus ride to Rockaway Beach, not really a beach but a glorified cesspool with sand, cigarette butts, transistor radios and all the women holding those three-fold metallic bits of cardboard meant to accentuate your tan, but eventually dismissed as causing premature aging and skin cancer. Judy was wearing cut-offs and a t-shirt that had a number written on it: 86. And this guy started to whisper, "Hey, 86, come here." We were sweltering, and the bus stank of petrol fumes and baby oil (everyone's tanning lotion of choice) and he kept saying. "86, 86, leave your kid friend and come here." Judy ignored him, and I said, "Hey, please can you leave us alone." And he said, "I am leaving you alone. You are the ugly friend. I want 86." Judy was loyal and ignored him and rolled her eyes at me, in that don't-you-hate-when-this-happens sort of way. Only it never happened to me, because I was a child and not a very attractive one.

Then it happened all at once just before I turned sixteen. I remember finding the blood on my pants (in Cutchogue) and ringing my mother. When I got back to the apartment in Queens, she went and fetched an old shoe box which contained a Kotex starter kit for young women. It was four years old and covered in dust. I remember her blowing the dust away, and the complication of the belts and blue lines and hooks and all the things that had, in the interim, been outdated by a new development which was stick-on pads. Everything about the kit was out of date. I said I wanted the stick-on pads, the new ones. But asking for them at the shop was an ordeal. I'd tag it onto the end of a family-sized packet of chewing-gum, a shampoo for my sister called Placenta Plus, Pepto Bismol, and yes, "a packet of these, please – for my mother". Girls used to clutch their stomachs in pain during their monthly periods, but mine hurt all the time anyway.

My stomach-aches got worse when I was fifteen or so, and that's when the doctors started to reel out heavier medications for me. They put me on a new type of anti-depressant called tricyclics, which I thought were specifically for kids because they sounded a bit like tricycle. For rather large chunks of time, I would not go to school at all, though I always kept up with my lessons. I imagined these little tricycles coursing around my veins, my understanding of neurological cause and effect very scant then, as it still is now. It boils down to: some pills make me feel better, some don't. Many years later I was to discover that I was hardcore addicted to the one that really made me feel better right away: Valium. It was, in later years, to be a large part of the undoing of me and what felt like a normal, happy life. I could not believe, when I grew up, that people took them for fun. "Charge sheets" they called them on the streets, where I eventually had to buy them. "Charge sheets" because, if you mixed them with drink (which I did), you could not remember what you had done the night before, until a friend (or ex-friend) read out your charges, what clubs you had been thrown out of, what toilets you had passed out in.

For most of my life, I just took them to feel normal. In some respects, I was pretty normal. I was an average student. I joined the school glee club. I was popular with girls because they liked me and with boys because there was nothing sexual about me – I was just a nice kid. A nice kid on heavy drugs, in the joyless glee club.

My sister and I started to bicker over the one thing that brought us together: pop music. She veered towards the new disco music, whereas I started to discover all the old stuff like Dylan, Joni Mitchell, Neil Young, Phil Ochs, the Stones, the Beatles, Richie Havens. I would study the lyrics for hours, finding new meaning in old words. She would study the new dance moves, and hit the discos, a blow-dried, blue-eye-shadowed blaze of polyester-clad, high-heeled sensuality. She had hordes of male admirers. Unlike me, she looked older than her age and knew all the make-up tricks to look grown up enough to get into a club. She looked spectacular in a halter-neck dress, which was the fashion at the time. The only way to stake my claim in our shared bedroom was to be as hippie as possible. I studied the accent of my friend's brother, who lived in Oregon, where he was something like a tree surgeon, a respectable hippie job. Every other word was "like" or "man". That was easy enough. I studied the loping gait of the New York City hippies, never in a hurry, always swinging their arms in a feel-good gesture. I wore bell-bottom jeans, which slid down my non-existent hips, and curly, frizzy hair that grew upwards, like that of folk singer Janis Ian, who was later to have a hit about realising she was ugly at seventeen. Even if you could not be conventionally pretty, which I was not, you could still be "yourself" and get away with it if you aligned yourself with the proper counterculture.

Strangely, in light of what I was to do to pay my rent

decades later, cleaning houses an ocean away, the rows I had with my sister usually ended with one or other of us destroying or breaking or messing up something the other one had put some sort of effort into; the key thing was to make a mess of something that had been acceptably tidy. That's how we fought. We messed each other's stuff up. These untidy-ings were minor misdemeanours in the scale of things, but there is nothing quite so purgative and anger-affirming as making a mess where order once existed. Rearranging or purposely mismatching or even getting rid of one of a pair of earrings on the obligatory teenage-girl-room-circa-mid-1970s earring tree. Wetting all the tips of the incense sticks. Unscrewing a lightbulb in the lighted make-up mirror. A common strategy was unmaking a made-up bed. Unfixing the fixed. Another was to scribble or draw over the pop star poster adorning the head-end of each of our beds. My sister once drew a big penis on my poster of Mick Jagger in his white flowing smock and drawstring trousers. So great was my embarrassment that the poster had to come down straightaway. My revenge? Spraying nearly the entire contents of a can of Raid cockroach killer on her bed, hoping she would guess that her bed had been invaded by the nocturnal creatures, but with the added moral one-upmanship that I was trying to save her from the roaches.

***

The mid-70s saw our little family of three spin off into different orbits. My mother was stepping out with a gentleman friend from time to time. My sister was lost in the disco craze, learning all the dances, getting into all the clothes, the make-up, the boys. I stayed at home most nights and played guitar or watched TV and did my homework well before it was due. Sometime during this period my sister ran away from home for a night or two. I think it was a dress rehearsal for moving out for good as soon as she was old enough. Unlike me, she couldn't wait to grow up. I came back from a friend's house, where I had been staying the night, to find cops at my kitchen table, going through my sister's schoolbooks and letters, looking for clues. They were looking through the copied-on-the-bus handwriting of her homework. My first thought was: is this a police crime, copying homework on the bus? She used to copy Spanish homework on the way into school. My mother told me gravely that my sister had "gone missing". It was passive. It was not that she had run away. She had gone missing. My second thought was, hurrah, that means I can have my own room. She returned one or two days later just as I was taking all her posters down. We never found out where she went, but I do remember admiring her loyalty. She never said who sheltered her. If she had stayed away long enough, she might have had her picture on the side of a milk carton. That's what they did. While you were having your Cheerios or Cap'n Crunch, you would see all these faces (mainly schoolbook photos with specs and braces) of missing kids. Maybe she would be famous enough missing to be on a milk carton. I could have my friends round for breakfast, pour the milk out and say, as if discovering it for the first time, "Holy cow! My sister is missing!"

When she was eighteen, my sister moved into an apartment around the corner, which she shared with airline hostesses. She had a good job as a secretary. Of the three of us, she seemed the most normal, functional one. She had beauty, charm, and quickly picked up all the dance steps that got you noticed at the disco. When I think back to the time when she was starting her first job, and I was still in school, I remember her slinking into some sexy dress, putting on her face in front of the make-up mirror, listening to the disco radio station and waving her pert arse in time to the music. I loved the glamour and independence she exuded, but I hated the music, the effort it took to straighten the hair, put on the face, get the shoes to match the dress. It was such a faff. It was far easier to be a hippie – though I did want to at least explore the other side.

Years later, when I was eighteen, I went up the avenue to the hairdressing parlour wedged between a health food shop and a travel agent. Get your fibre supplements, a blow-dry and plan a trip to the Bahamas. The guy who cut and blow-dried my hair chatted non-stop: How old was I? Was this the first time I got my hair cut? Did I like his medallion? I wanted to know if life would be different with straight hair.

"Do you want wings?" he asked. He meant like Farrah Fawcett.

"Sure, wings will be fine."

When he was done, I stared in the mirror at this stranger. She looked like me, but even uglier, with straighter hair, and wings. I burst into tears.

"Why are you crying? You look beautiful. Look. I live just a short drive away. You wanna smoke a joint, relax? I have some great records; what are you into?"

Mechanically, I paid the cashier and, robot-like, still puffy-faced from crying, I climbed into his car. He slipped a cassette into the tape player. Barry White. Groaning. We were at his apartment before the song was over. He had a complicated sofa, which took up the whole living-room. It was called "the Pit", and you could arrange the different pieces in all sorts of ways, but the main thing to do on "the Pit" was to lie down. We smoked a joint. Well, he did; I pretended to. I didn't like it. My perception was altered enough by the stronger stuff I got from the doctor. I knew at some point he would want sex. I had had sex before, made love, that is to say, with my boyfriend. I found it a messy, painful business but it seemed to be the thing to do, if you had a boyfriend. I figured it would get better as I got older and learned how to do it.

We went into his bedroom, his bed made up with masculine-patterned sheets, darkness and light, broad stripes, a brocaded bedspread.

He said, "As soon as I saw your tits I knew I had to have you."

I had only very recently acquired them. If this is what they got me – brocade, bad music and, what I came to realise later, rape – I felt I was better off without them.

I said, "I don't want to have a baby. A blow-dried baby, conceived to Barry White." He had removed the tape from his car and put it in his home stereo system.

He laughed, smelled my chemical hair and stuck his

thing into me sharply, painfully. Between the "My" and the "God" it was all over. We got dressed quickly so he could get back for his "three o'clock". He told me not to tell anyone. He said, "Wait, I have to fix your hair." He sprayed and moussed and blow-dried me some more. I was mute. He said, "Just a little fun. You really are eighteen, right?"

Cleaning, London 2015
THE INTERVIEW

IN 2015, I GO FOR an interview at a cleaning agency. I go armed with a fake CV and two gushing letters, written by my friends, about what a "treasure" I am and how meticulous I am. I have to edit one of the letters to make it sound more real.

I have not had a formal job interview since I was 23. I have forgotten how they go. The kids seem to bang on a lot about being passionate about… whatever it is they are applying for. I rehearse this. "I am passionate about cleaning." No, doesn't sound authentic. I am passionate about cleansing. Oh God, no. Wait... I am not wishy-washy about washing. Nah, too clever clogs. I think I need to play my stupid card, which comes naturally to me.

Right now, the biggest appeal about cleaning is that it is a job I can do with minimal human communication. I have recently come off drink and drugs, and I have forgotten the nuances of social interaction. I want to do something mechanically, without much thought. And it's a nice thing to do for other people. It's nice to come home to a clean house or flat. I want to be someone's treasure.

The interview is conducted by a handsome young man with a rictus grin and an air of desperation. I have the feeling I could be an axe murderer and still get the gig. His phone rings non-stop during the interview and little sweat patches are forming under his crumply pink shirt.

"I could press that shirt for you if you like."

"No, you don't understand," he says patiently. "You will not be *my* cleaner. You will clean for lots of people, but not me."

"Yeah, I know, it was just banter."

"Oh right… ha ha ha".

He asks what I think are the qualities that make a good cleaner.

I say, "Attention to detail."

"Perfect. Exactly. It's all in the details."

He shows me a picture of the agency's "Cleaner of the Month". The guy looks sort of Turkish, heavy-set, walrus moustache, big smile, olive skin and hairy arms.

I have to stifle a memory-jogging giggle. This cleaner of the month looks exactly like a guy I used to see in an advert on the NYC subway: "Armando Vargas: Haemorrhoid Sufferer". Smiling because he found relief in such-and-such cooling cream for piles. My sister's friend Yvonne used to rip the posters down on rush-hour trains and explain, in a fake Puerto Rican accent: "Dios mío Uncle Armando bringing shame on all the family."

The guy can see I am trying not to laugh and says, "What? What's so funny?"

I could tell him about the subway and Uncle Armando but it is so far from his universe or anything we are here to talk about. I can tell him it's a long story, but I feel I'm already in danger of messing this up. I just ask him how you get to be cleaner of the month, to be the poster girl.

The guy leans in as if he's telling me one of those trade secrets, like, "If you tell anyone, I'll have to kill you. No one knows this."

"At the end of a clean," he says, "the cleaner gets into the bathtub, which he has dried. He looks at the walls of the bathroom from a person-in-the-bath's point of view. He can see streak marks, hairs, maybe a toenail he's missed, or soap residue at the back end of a tap or" – here he leans in a little further – "the dreaded London limescale."

I nod. "Right. Detail".

I picture myself doing this bathtub trick. I picture a young lad, perhaps my son's age, coming into the bathroom, flipping up the toilet seat and having a wee. From the corner of his eye he'll see me but act nonchalant.

"Hey."

"Hey."

"Uh, what are you doing?"

"Checking for toenails and limescale."

"Cool."

"Oi."

"What?"

"Flush and put the loo seat down, please."

I will be a natural.

They hire me. They would have hired anyone. My first wage slip is two quid for a two-hour clean. They call this a finder's fee. I have been found.

Chapter Four

In the mid-70s, my mother got a new cleaner. Betty was Hispanic and had a long commute in from New Hersey, as she pronounced it. She became a good friend to my mother and the supposed cleaning sessions were mainly Betty and my mother having a good old chinwag over instant coffee and cigarettes. Betty was mad for cats and had enough to qualify her as a crazy cat lady. We only had the one, Suki, a loud, neurotic Siamese, afraid of everyone except the immediate family and Betty. When Betty wasn't chatting to my mum or drinking coffee or smoking, she was playing with the cat. The fact that the apartment never looked much different from before she came to after she'd left was neither here nor there. She was a companion and she made my mother happy. Plus, she eventually got my mother to pay in cash after telling her that it took too long to "put the money in my cunt, Mrs Joyce". My mother spent the next few minutes explaining the difference between cunt and account.

Years later my mother got her first bout of cancer and Betty would come with all sorts of strange purées for Mrs Joyce, who could barely eat, to swallow. She was loyal, fiercely so, and I believe a sort of love existed between her and my mother. She'd measure my mother's progress by making the purées slightly lumpier, the way they do with jars of baby food. I don't think my mother could stomach the purées, smooth or lumpy, but she loved Betty and would tell her they were delicious. Betty told my mother this job was much nicer than her old job. She had been a nurse who had to assist in abortions. She had seen enough. Now, she just wanted to smoke and chat and drink instant coffee and clean the counter tops. She had one bottle of cleaner for every job. Pure ammonia. It cut through everything and made our eyes water. This was a sign that the flat had been Bettied, neat ammonia poured on lino that had not been replaced since the 60s. She kept cat treats in her bag for Suki. She called the treats "cookies" and would beckon Suki over to her handbag, fishing out the baggie of cookies. Mum was happy. The cat was happy. The flat was germ-free to a near-toxic degree.

Later, Betty got cancer and my mother did the same for her, travelling out to New Hersey and trying to tempt Betty with spoonfuls of baby food.

The introduction of Betty coincided with my last few years of secondary school. During those years, I felt something approaching happy, though I was still on prescription drugs, some for the stomach, some for the head, along with the ones I liked best, the "Just in case" ones for free-floating terror. "Take as Needed", the three magic words on any prescription sheet. On the way to school I would get myself a coffee from the candy store/luncheonette and a *New York Times* from the newsstand. The back section had a summary, so you could find out everything that was happening in the world while spilling coffee and bumping into people. Pretty pilled up but pretty high functioning, I started to explore life outside school, outside my neighbourhood.

My first port of call was Greenwich Village: last bastion of the dying breed of hippies. In Washington Square Park they would gather near the fountain or on the dried-up bits of summer grass. They had long hair and were often filthy and many of them carried guitars on their backs. They were buskers, playing anything that would draw a crowd: the Beatles, Neil Young, James Taylor, Carole King, the Grateful Dead. One guy had been part of the original Youth International Party, which has stood for something at some time and I believe elected a pig, a real pig, for some election. Whatever was going on in the modern world, they were not for it. They felt everyone should just smoke dope and make love. I was terrified of dope as it was not prescribed, and I had no feeling for sex, but I liked the hippie look – it seemed low maintenance – and I liked that they befriended me even though I looked about twelve. I started to bring my guitar, too, and played along with the hippie buskers. Not all of the songs came easily to me, so I asked my mother to take me to Sam Goody, the big music store, to buy sheet music.

I chose the Eagles songbook. My mother flicked through it and stumbled on the song "Peaceful Easy Feeling" and read out loud, in her louder, angrier English accent, "I want to sleep with you in the desert tonight…" Then she said, "I don't want you singing songs about dirty hippies having sex in the desert." And I said, "It's not sex, it's sleeping. Anyway, it's just a song. I promise you, I swear, if you buy this songbook I won't have sex in the desert with a hippie." But she was unwavering in her decision that Eagles songbooks led to promiscuity in deserts with dirty hippies and besides, when and if you do have sex, it should be in a bed with your husband, not in a desert where you can get sand you-know-where and where there's not a glass of water to drink afterwards. I put down the Eagles songbook and decided if I couldn't play along on a particular song, I would bob my head in a meaningful fashion and say, "Yeah, man" at various intervals.

The guy from the Youth International Party, David Peel, was less of a singer, more of a shouter. He drew a big crowd and his main thing seemed to be about legalising pot. It was the last dying cause of the Yippies. One day there was a march up Fifth Avenue and all the Yippie leftovers and little hangers-on like me walked from Washington Square to Central Park, where there was to be a rally. I felt anxiety-free. David Peel kept shouting, "A pot in every chicken!" as the hippies laughed and said, "Far out! The dude's right." I liked these angry pot smokers, how they were desperately clinging onto a time that no longer existed. This motif was familiar to me. Cling onto something that no longer exists. A feeling, a father, the past. I asked one girl, her arms covered entirely with bangles and a little jewel stuck to the middle of her forehead, what it was all about: "Well, little sister, we wanna get stoned, when we want, where we want."

"But then how would you do the stuff you have to do, like work, stuff like that?"

"Wooah, sister's getting all heavy. You like a narc, in disguise? Haha, far out."

"No, I just want to know what it feels like to…"

And here she grabbed my arm and said, "C'mon, we gotta go. We're going to Central Park. Once we get there they're dropping thousands of joints from a helicopter. It'll turn you on, but we gotta go before it all runs out."

We linked arms and marched up the street, cops all over the place, mainly on horseback. At one point they cordoned us off and some of the hippies and Yippies burst through the cordon and those who knew me said, "Come on, Michele, you can do it, you're little, you can go under the horses." I ran for it and got kicked by a horse. It hurt like hell, but I did make it through the barrier and on to the rally in Central Park. I remember losing interest in the prospect of thousands of joints falling from the sky and my shin was throbbing from where the horse kicked me, so I left the park and got the subway back to Queens. I was hoping it would be in the next day's papers. I was hoping there would not be a photograph of the horse kicking me, but I was also kind of hoping that there would be. It would prove I cared about something, even though I didn't care about what they cared about.

I also got a boyfriend. He was of the hippie tribe and smelled like dope and patchouli oil. He wore clothing generally regarded as "ethnic". Usually miles too big for him. We were two skinny stalks, topped by unruly curly, frizzy hair. I had found my soul mate, my hair twin.

We had no money, so we did not go on dates. We'd walk around the neighbourhood and find a park bench and sit down on it and kiss. Sometimes he came back to my mother's apartment, but she watched us like a hawk. He used to do this very annoying thing of asking strangers for cigarettes. I said, "Don't do that with me. It makes you look like a beggar." He promised he would never do it again but then a guy came towards us smoking a cigarette and he said, "Excuse me, sir, may I have a cigarette?" and the guy said sure and even lit it for him. I knew then that I had no power over this man, who my best friend called "Dusty in the Wind", after a popular song on the radio which we all learned to play on guitar. Dusty was dirty. Dirty fingernails, an unwashed smell, despite the lashings of patchouli. I just figured it was one of those hippie things you had to put up with and once you stopped going out with hippies, your boyfriends would be cleaner.

My next boyfriend was a hippie from Washington Square Park, where the last of the hippies all hung out. I can't remember his name, but I do remember he read poetry to me and had a beard, which I thought was very grown up. Again, on some park bench, late at night, he grabbed my hand and thrust it down his trousers. What *was* this shit, with men and their trousers? I said, "What the fuck are you doing?" He breathed that he wanted me to touch him. And I said, "Down there???" and he nodded desperately, and I said, "But that's private. And I would not want to invade your privacy." A line that took him by surprise. He said, "Please! Invade my privacy!!!" I couldn't bring myself to do it, and decided to give up on boys and concentrate on reading. Books never grabbed your hands and stuck them down their trousers. They didn't try to unhook your bra with one hand. They didn't make weird noises. Books and newspapers: you could learn so much, without all the nonsense of touching and being touched.

I particularly liked a paper called the *Soho Weekly News*, which was covering the growing art scene in Soho, which was on the cusp of gentrification. I remember there was a difficulty in getting that paper in Queens, when I was seventeen and an avid reader, so I took it upon myself to go to the offices in Spring Street, Soho, and set up a subscription for myself.

The office was a glorious mess. Some of the staff looked like hippies and some of them looked like punks. Most people sat at typewriters, papers all over the place, overflowing ashtrays, half-empty coffee cups. It was less of an office, more of a disorderly maze, every door leading to some strange nook or cranny or whole other room, back in the days when computers took up entire walls. I started to ask the receptionist who was responsible for circulation, and she gestured to the far end of the office. A large guy called Michael, the editor of the paper, came up to me and said, "Are you the new girl? The intern?" It seemed too good an opportunity to miss, this mistaken identity. What would happen if I lied? It could be an adventure. I nodded, and Michael called out, "Buzzy, your girl is here!" and then he ushered me to a back room. The door was closed. I went in, and found a room with two desks, a calculator and every back issue of the paper stacked up on industrial metal shelving. I couldn't find the man, Buzzy. He was hiding behind a door, sucking what I thought was oxygen from a metal canister. He was dressed like an undertaker and was attractively wolverine. He peered at me up and down, which made me nervous. I fished a Valium out of my bag and he was on to me right away. "What's that you got there? Valium? How many? Can you get more? We must have as many as possible. The election is looking bad. We will need at least four years' worth."

I told him I would see what I could do about the pills. My first assignment as a would-be journalist: get my boss four years' worth of medication. I never found out what was in the canister, but I believe it was some sort of dental laughing gas. Except Buzzy never laughed.

That summer I was seventeen was a typical humid, stinkingly hot NYC summer. The only relief was the occasional rainstorm, when a strange smell would emerge from the pavements, a mixture of old dog piss and discarded bits of hot dogs and body odour. The smell was so bad and only relieved by the rain, which came hard and fast and horizontally. You just knew it would be like this, stiflingly hot and humid, or pissing down at intervals, from mid-May to mid-September. My mother escaped to Liverpool. My sister was already set up in a studio apartment not far from where my mother lived.

Every morning I got on the train and went to the offices in Soho, hoping I would not be found out but sort of knowing they wouldn't care anyway. If I timed the pill right I would be feeling pretty good by the time the E train pulled into Jackson Heights. From there the journey was about another 45 minutes.

Once I was at the office, I made jobs for myself. Buzzy was usually on the phone, or working with his calculator and ledger. I put all the back issues in order. I took subscriptions over the phone. I liked to hang about the music desk, where all the cool-looking people congregated. They played a strange, discordant music that I was later to learn was called No Wave. It was angular, angry and hard to listen to. I liked it. It made me feel alive, which was not that easy, as I was munching so much Valium. The doctors had given me more, on request, and I learned not to take them in front of people, because then they would ask me for some. It never occurred to me that people just couldn't get their own. I had already lied to Buzzy and told him my doctor wouldn't give me any more.

One morning, I got a call from Buzzy to tell me the circulation department had caught fire. The fireman had said it was safe to go back in and could I go in and start to sort out the mess. I was strangely excited. I had never been in a space that had been on fire before. I imagined it would be terribly messy and full of soot and burnt things, and to make it nice and clean again seemed the decent thing to do.

I let myself in, that morning after the fire. The front looked normal, but as I went towards the back the smell hit me. The smell of burnt newspapers is not so bad. It smells a bit like a fire you would make on purpose, in a fireplace, or on bonfire night, or when camping. But, when I got into the office itself, all romantic notions of saving the day would have flown out the window, had there been one. The firemen had hosed down most of the room, including the newspapers, which were swollen to double or even treble their size by the water and stuck between the shelves. I tried to pull one issue out but it would not budge. Eventually it came out in pieces, in lumps and hunks of torn newspaper, of torn words.

I rang Buzzy. I told him, "It's worse than you can imagine. The shelves are stuffed with stuck, wet newspaper. Nothing will budge."

He paused. Then, "Do you have a screwdriver?"

"Oh sure, that's just the sort of thing I carry on me. It's somewhere in my bag next to the Pepto Bismol and Compazine and Valium."

"Do you have drugs?"

"Of course, just get here. Bring soda or coffee. This is going to take a long time."

Buzzy showed up about two hours later and just held out his hand for his medicine. We both dropped a couple of Vs and soon we were pulling odd, torn issues out of the steel shelves, very, very slowly. We read bits out to each other. All afternoon we spent like this, drinking cold coffee, pulling out shreds of paper, trying to make a dustpan out of a piece of cardboard and a brush out of some dry newspapers. It was terrible, in that no matter what we did, the room would still look as if there had been a fire. A lot of our back issues were destroyed. Those that remained were waterlogged or stuck fast to the shelves, which Buzzy started to dismantle with his screwdriver. We'd throw some stuff out, saying, "Shame, that was a good issue," and others we would joyfully tip into one of the many bin bags we had open.

"This is like *Fahrenheit 451*," I said.

"No, it's not as important as that. Let's leave this and grab a beer."

My very first cleaning job was abandoned, for the impossibility of it. We went down to the Lower East Side and into some no-name bar and he got two beers and drank both of them. He also got a brandy for me, which tasted disgusting, but I downed it and it felt like medicine, the warmth trickling down my gullet into my coffee-swashing stomach. The combination of Valium and spirits was a revelation. Everything suddenly felt possible and wonderful, in a woozy, woolly-headed sort of way. I felt calm, wise and portentous. Everything that had never made sense suddenly made sense. Drugs and a little drink made me feel, at seventeen, like the King God of all wisdom. I told Buzzy I didn't want to work in circulation any more. I wanted to write. "You know, I really like newspapers. Even burnt ones. Even the ones swollen with firehose water. I think I want to be a journalist when I grow up."

Buzzy did not nod. He looked me squarely in the eye and grabbed my shoulders. He said, "No, you really don't. You want to be something more noble. I want you to be something more noble." He finished my brandy and continued, "To be a journalist in this day and age is to be a wasted form, the lowest form, of protoplasmic life. I think you should be a schoolteacher. They are noble."

I promised him I would. I cursed the fire and the drink and the solemnity it gave my already cadaverous friend, and we weaved our way towards Avenue B, near where he lived with his girlfriend, in a shell of a building. The Lower East Side, back then, was where you lived if you had no money. Nobody, except the editor on the paper, had much money, but everyone seemed to really like what they did. Nobody gave the impression that working on newspapers was actually work. That is what I wanted to do: to spend my grown-up life working in a place that didn't feel like work. Cleaning most certainly did feel like work, but it would be an age before I started doing it for money. Once, the editor came raging through the office, his face tomato-red, and shouted, "Everyone clean up your stuff. The publisher is coming." He grabbed me and told me to tidy the desk of one of the journalists who was not there: a brilliant writer with a very messy desk. I didn't even know where to begin. The editor steered me over and picked up what looked like green tobacco leaves and tiny little peppercorns. "Get rid of anything that looks like this," he said. "Don't get rid of it – just put it all in a bag and stick it in the back of his filing cabinet."

Even with fingernails and swift hands, I found the job took ages. Despite the pot march, despite people smoking it all around me, I had never really touched the stuff so I had no notion of what I was handling. I remember thinking, what is the deal with this guy and all these goddamn peppercorns?

Cleaning, London 2015
OFFICES

OFFICE CLEANS ARE VERY SPECIFIC. You have to decide what is garbage and what is not. If it's an empty or near-empty food container it is garbage. If it's a pad with lots of squiggles on it, it is not, and you have to dust or clean around it. I'm doing a big office, three floors of various start-up businesses. No matter how late I get there, or how early, there is always some start-up whizz in their early 20s or late teens, talking on their phone, skyping, drawing huge mind maps with seemingly unrelated thoughts, but actually all to do with selling something maybe ethical, or something people in the modern world need. Spices for dinner, pre-measured. Handcream that lasts 24 hours. The perfectly planned wedding. There is a small kitchen area, touchingly filled with sugar-coated kiddie cereals. To my middle-aged eyes, these kids are still babies. Mainly, I drag a giant wet and dry vacuum cleaner up and down flights of stairs, picking up empty Pret and Wasabi containers on the way. One kid's desk is cluttered with empty energy drinks and sweet packets. He is on the phone just as I switch the vacuum cleaner on and he gesticulates with a cut sign to his throat, pointing dramatically at the phone. How dare he, I think. Look at your life, you should be out clubbing; it's night time, you should be with your gal, or your guy, or at home watching telly as your mum makes your tea. But here you are, sugared up, talking up a storm to someone from God knows where who will relent and buy whatever it is you are selling, and you are seventeen.

Maybe he looks at me and thinks, my mother is younger than she is. She must be a halfwit, to be a cleaner. A bit English-as-a-second-language-y. Why isn't she at home, making dinner with pre-measured spices, delivered to her door?

I turn off the machine and for a second I am sure we glance at each other, both of us thinking, *"You poor fucker"*.

Chapter Five

Everybody I liked seemed to live on the Lower East Side, a neighbourhood with so many broken-down gaps between the tenements that it was like a giant mouth in need of major dentistry. Kids used to play on the rubble between buildings. There were rats as big as cats, and if you walked down certain streets, you'd see queues of ill, thin-looking people standing outside a building. Some dealers had rigged up a pulley system with a string and basket; you'd put the money in the basket, they'd haul it up, and send the drugs down in the basket. Fearless and stupid, I asked one guy what was in the basket, what everyone was lining up for.

"Candy."

"Why don't you just go to the candy store?"

"This is the candy store."

I made no connection between their candy and the "candy" that rattled around my bag. Heroin was, like, proper drugs. I was just necking Benzos. All very civilised: saw my man once a month, lush apartment on the Upper East Side. Beautiful manners. French accent. He had a doorman. That was a true sign of social success, a doctor on the Upper East Side with a doorman, a fat prescription pad and legible handwriting. He checked my vitals, he brought out his wonderful pad, scribbled and gave me a sheet. I would then go back to Queens and give the sheet to Mario, the drugstore guy. Did I want to wait, or did I want it delivered? No, I'd wait. I loved the sound of the rattle in my bag, calming the rattle of my brain and stomach. I remember once comparing bag contents with one of my girlfriends. Hers contained a lipstick, a spare packet of Hanes pantyhose, a bottle of Charlie perfume, keys and a fake ID. Mine was just full of brown bottles of pills, and keys.

Quietly and efficiently and legally sedated, I made friends at the paper and went to strange parties. A tall, gangly, handsome guy came over to me one day in the office and shyly asked if I would like to get some food in Chinatown. I wasn't sure what he did at the paper. He seemed very good at fixing anything that was broken, and his mother worked in typesetting. I said yes, and me and the guy's mother, still a friend of mine today, all went to Chinatown.

We started dating. We used to go to a bar in the West Village called Chumleys. It had a private entrance. We'd have a glass of wine each and whatever else he could afford, which was not all that much. I always wanted money for the jukebox. He used words most people didn't use any more, like "nifty" for cool, and he had the most happy-go-lucky gait. If someone walks happy, I like them right away. Big swinging arms, loping from side to side, more striding than walking. Sometimes I think of him still and find myself walking the way he used to walk, in giant, happy steps. My mother nicknamed him Pale and Tortured but there was nothing tortured about him except me.

I lived so far away but my boyfriend would take me on the crosstown bus to the West Village and sometimes get on the train with me back to Queens. It was a very long round trip for one lingering kiss in front of the door. I thought about him all the time. In school, out of school; something in me was stirring, but I had no name for it. I can't really remember what we did or where we went, but as we had no privacy, it was impossible to explore this longing. There were always loads of children and their friends where he lived, and there was always the shadowy presence of my mother in our apartment. She would come into the living room at regular intervals to make sure all was as it should be. At his place, you went up some stairs and were greeted with a black-and-white painting of Kafka with one eye gouged out. From there, cats would leap from bookcases onto your shoulder, a dog with a chronic ear infection would sniff around your feet, and whichever room you found yourself in, you'd be greeted with loving enthusiasm by a collection of children and animals.

Downstairs, the bar jukebox probably had more than one song, but all anyone ever put a quarter in for was Gloria Gaynor's "I Will Survive". The bassline would vibrate through the floorboards, and after a while you found yourself doing things in time to the beat.

Around September or October of 78, I had to start applying for colleges. There was one I liked in Boston. My boyfriend was going to meet me there and we would have the weekend together. A friend of his offered us the use of her apartment, and we went up to Boston. Me on the plane, him on the train. I remember little about the apartment, except that the woman who lived there and loaned it to us left him a note with smiley faces, which made me think she had been a former girlfriend. Was she beautiful? Had they done what we were about to do?

The apartment itself seemed to be in a state of packing-up. Everything was in boxes. So, we lay on a sleeping bag on the floor and fumbled and kissed and that longing feeling, so nice in my head, turned into a sort of blind panic now that something certainly was going to happen. When it did, I felt the expected pain, but also a deep sense of love and contentment and a feeling that, with practice, though I couldn't imagine where or when this would happen, this would be something I would come to enjoy.

The next morning, I had my interview for the college. I felt I had nothing to say except that I had gone to Boston a girl and was now a woman but, even with my lack of filter in formal situations, I knew I could not really expand on this theme to my interviewers. They asked me all sorts of things about myself, my interests, what I read, what I liked, what I thought of various world events. All I could think of was, "I've had sex. Not even on drugs." But I understood implicitly that this was not the answer to any of the questions. I stared out the window on to the tree-lined street and was asked something about life experience. I leaned forward and said, "You know, I've had a few experiences. I really like my weekend job on this newspaper. But I've had other experiences."

"Tell me about one of them."

"I can't." I wanted to say the worst thing that ever happened to me was by accident. That was my father getting killed. The best thing that ever happened to me was by accident. I went into a newspaper and they thought I had come to work, but actually I had come to ask a question. It turned into one of the most fun summers of my life. And it led to me falling in love. With a profession. With a man as well, who was walking around the grounds somewhere.

I got into the college. The boyfriend, frustrated by circumstance and limitations, moved to California. I was bereft. He wrote me letters. I listened to sad music and wrote letters back. I knew life in California was better for him, then, than on the Lower East Side.

In September, I was ready, but actually not ready at all, to move to Boston to start college. I was still on a lot of prescription drugs and could pretend to be normal, if the situation warranted it. Nothing in my body seemed to work without adding something else. Not food, not belonging, not a sense of purpose. It had to come in a brown plastic pill bottle, and it had to have my name on it, and it had to have those magic words "Take as needed". My stomach was in such rebellion that sometimes it was hard even to swallow the pills. To combat this nausea and keep the pills down, I was given suppositories. It was in this medicated haze that I got into the passenger seat of my sister's ex-boyfriend's car and we started the long drive to Boston.

He gave me a talking-to as we rode up the highway listening to Hendrix. Don't mess with boys, don't mess with drugs, don't change, you're a good girl, work hard, you can be something, you can be anything. It was that sort of thing. He told me I was almost as pretty as my sister, only almost, but that was OK because I had personality and some guys dug that.

I didn't bother to tell him that I had already messed with a boy and I was chock full of drugs or that, as they were all legal, and the messing with the boy bit had been an act of love, I felt my moral slate was clean. He told a lot of rambling stories, some of which I enjoyed. He had been in the Marines and had lots of stories about that.

"You know how they teach you to swim in the Marines?"

"No."

"They throw you in. Then you swim. Or start drowning."

"What did you do?"

"I did a little of both."

He then told me how to make a bed in the Marines, how to polish your shoes in the Marines, how to exercise for hours in the Marines, how to take ritual humiliation in the Marines, how to fight in the Marines, how not to get thrown out of the Marines and so on. I think none of the stories had much of a point, except to make me less afraid of going to college, compared to the Marines.

When we got to the dorms, he helped me unpack and left. My room-mates arrived, one from the south, going to the drama school, and one from the Midwest, studying... well, she wasn't sure yet. I unpacked by putting all my punk posters on the side of the wall that was closest to my bed and getting out my record player and playing this No Wave music. Mainly a song called "Too Many Creeps". It made me immediately homesick for New York. I lined up all my pill bottles on my desk, around my new electric typewriter. Stomach suppositories here, nerve pills there, depression pills by the stack of paper, over-the-counter stomach remedies as a just-in-case gesture.

Then something very strange happened. I've since read about other cases, but only after people have terrible head injuries. They wake up speaking a new language or with an impenetrable foreign accent. I was lying on my bed, playing air bass to "Too Many Creeps", and one of my room-mates introduced herself, and I said, "Alright, then?" in a totally fake cockney accent. I thought, who said that? Was it a strange side effect of the many pills I was popping? We had a little chat, the whole time me speaking in this, now that I think of it, really bad cockney accent. It would have been too strange to suddenly break out of it, back into my New Yorkese. I was half-British but had spent most of my life in New York. I had not earned this accent. I had not put in the geographical time. If I were to have any sort of English accent, it should have been Scouse. It was totally fake. Even a mid-Atlantic accent would have been pushing it; the only people who could get away with that sort of thing were gay men who worked on the cosmetic counters of posh department stores. In hindsight it seemed a good way of not being me and, if I were not me, I would not be anxious. But the rules of anxiety don't work like that.

So, I was stuck, in a new state, in a new school, with a new accent. The only thing that remained the same were my drugs. I think it was an attempt at total reinvention with pharmaceutical assistance. I was to dive in and out of this accent over the next few years, with varying degrees of success. It did not change anything else about me. The anxiety I suffered from was a permanent fixture. I was forever running out of lectures to gulp in the fresh air and throw some pills down my throat and shove a suppository up the other end. I would stumble back to my room, try to read my lecture notes and fall into a sort of semi-sedated fog. It was an unhappy time for me. I made friends; I was the sort of English-but-not-really girl on drugs she never shared. As in New York, my sense of real danger was totally blunted by my imaginary sense of impending doom.

One day when I took a long walk and found myself in a part of Boston that looked like the Lower East Side, this guy started walking in step with me. He started chatting about this and that. "You one of 'em college girls?"

"I guess so, yeah."

"You wanna get high?"

"Well, thing is, see, I don't really…"

"Come on, sugar, come get high with me."

My street smarts had gone right out of the window with my natural accent. I was courting danger, big time. When you are so consumed with free-floating anxiety, there is very little sense of proper danger. Anxiety and recklessness seem to make strange bedfellows – you are so stuck on your inner feelings that you have little sense of what is actually going on around you.

He lit up a joint, right there in the street, took a long drag and passed it to me. I put it between my lips and sucked the smoke into my mouth. It tasted terrible. I could not inhale it. I coughed it out and he laughed.

The streets, which were unfamiliar anyway, were disappearing, and we were in the middle of a housing project. Just loads of buildings with broken windows, garbage cans on fire and zigzags of fire escapes. He said we should go see a friend of his, so I followed him up the stairs; and then the friendliness stopped. He unzipped his flies and pulled out his thing, springing to angry, expectant life, and pushed my head right down. I had no idea what to do. I said, "Look, mister, I..."

"C'mon, sister, I got you high, you think you can get somethin' for nothin'? White whore. White college whore. Do what you gotta do."

I started to shout and suddenly a man in a vest came out of his apartment, pulled me up and into his apartment and threw me against the wall.

"You dumb-ass motherfucker! You crazy white bitch. What you thinking?"

The other guy was pounding on the door. The guy in the apartment picked up a knife and opened the door on a chain. "You want to get cut, nigga? Get outta my apartment building, NOW!"

He turned back to me. "Some people have no sense, man, no sense at all. You crazy or what?"

"I, uh…"

"Don't come round here no more. Get your white ass back to wherever you from and don't come round here no more."

I ran out of the apartment and back to the dorm. It took a long time. After that I couldn't sleep for three days, so the "house mother", a graduate student who looked after the freshmen, took me to a doctor. The doctor gave me a great knock-out pill and that was that. I never told anyone about it because I felt so stupid. The panic attacks got worse and I would wake up to swallow a mouthful of drugs, would take them throughout the day and go to sleep with them at night.

Within a semester I had dropped out, unable to attend classes on a regular basis, unable to eat, unable to sleep, despite all the sedation. Going back to New York didn't feel right. The paper I loved so much was about to fold. I moved into a sublet in Boston for the summer. I had social security (payments connected with the death of my father) and I found a low-cost mental health centre, and spent the summer experimenting with stronger prescription drugs, experiencing bizarre side effects from the stomach medicine, including my legs suddenly giving way in a sort of shaking spasm and an inability to write in a legible hand and, sometimes, an inability to talk, my tongue feeling twice its size, getting in the way of syllables and vowels. It was just as well. It helped me sometimes avoid the accidental English accent. By this time I was not only shoving the anti-nausea drug up my bottom, but also swigging it in liquid form from a bottle.

It was called Compazine. It was a terrible drug to take while wearing complicated footwear – I was a slave to a type of high-heeled sandals called Candies and crossing Commonwealth Avenue, where the overground train rails ran flush with the road, was fraught with heel-catching danger. I remember once falling, feeling a shaking fit coming on, right on the train tracks. OK, this is it, I thought, the "T", as it was called, is going to come and run me over. But some old lady came over from the pavement and helped me up. She said, "Are you intoxicated?" I was trying to get the words out that, no, I was not intoxicated, I was on medication. She brought me back to my flat and started to pray for me. She was a Jehovah's Witness. I sat on my sofa, shaking, wishing she would leave, thinking, now they pick people off the rails. I thought they used to just knock on doors.

There were many episodes like that. Strangers coming to my rescue. When I had a job in a laundrette, I had a massive panic attack and had to ring the boss to get someone else in. On the shaky walk home, I fell over and could not seem to get myself up. A stranger came over and tried to lift me, but I said I would be OK. He didn't believe me and rang an ambulance. They took me to an emergency room and looked me over and told me I was having a panic attack. A few weeks later, I got a huge hospital bill. Churches or hospital rooms – these were the places well-meaning folk took me. I didn't mind the Jehovah's Witnesses so much because when they were not rescuing me from the tram tracks, they knocked on the door and came in and prayed for me. Jehovah's Witnesses might be the only people an agoraphobic talks to all day. It's a great religion for people who don't like to leave the house.

These rescues did not strike me as abnormal, but they were largely unwelcome. I just needed to figure out the right dose of medicine, enough to settle my stomach and head, but not so much as to give me the shakes. I was also lucky in that I had got myself a boyfriend whose brother was a pharmacist. He used to get me the pills that I wanted that were just about to go out of date. I had drugs literally going into and out of the two main orifices of the digestive tract. On the days I could not make it out of bed, I used to joke to myself that it was a "bad day at the orifice". It never occurred to me that I had a drug problem or, as it was later rebranded when I got into formal recovery, a "spiritual malady". I just needed this shit like other people needed food.

My problem, as put to me by various medical professionals, was that I had a chronic anxiety disorder. My drugs problem was that I could never seem to get enough of them.

My view was that nature and nurture had conspired to make me terrified of everything and, though this was unfortunate, there were drugs to balance it all out, and make life more or less doable. As time went on, and my hunger for drugs increased in inverse proportion to my hunger for food, it sometimes struck me that my solution was becoming my main problem. Not often, but sometimes.

I read up a lot about agoraphobia. I found a self-help

group about a 20-minute bus ride from where I was living and somehow made it to the first meeting. There were only two other people there. Most of the meeting was taken up by the chair announcing apologies for all the people who could not attend. "Apologies from Frances, from David, from Georgia, from Ellen…" This was before the advent of mobile phones so the pay phone in the meeting hallway was always ringing, and one of us would get up to answer it and it would be someone explaining, tearfully, that they had made it to the bus stop, felt dizzy and sick and ran back home.

The other thing I noticed about this first self-help group was that the chairs were set up in a circle, which is a common seating plan for self-help groups, and that the three, four or five people who attended immediately moved seats to be on those closest to the door, which is a very agoraphobic thing to do. The best seat in the house is the one you can get out of the quickest. I still live by this principle.

Cleaning, London 2015
FLATSHARES

I CLEAN FLATSHARES WITH A heavy heart. Usually but not always they are badly built, falling-to-bits flats in council tower blocks or other ex-council housing, where the only communal space is the kitchen – the "lounge" long ago converted to another bedroom. Usually there is one sleepy-eyed or hungover night worker to let me in and show me what needs doing, or an early starter, gulping coffee, checking his or her emails, impatient to get out.

These flats give me the illusion of superpower strength, for anything I touch or try to open breaks, or comes away in my hand. I open a kitchen cupboard to clean up a turmeric spillage, and the whole door falls off. I try to put it back where it belongs, turmeric fingerprints staining everything I touch. I realise this is what everyone does. They put things back in the general direction of where they belong, knowing that the next person who opens it will blame themselves. This charade goes on, and nothing gets mended. I leave the kitchen, praying the door won't fall off entirely, and head for the bathroom in a slow, Bionic Woman run. It's not that the cupboard is weak, I tell myself, but that I am super-strong.

I am asked to clean the main bedroom, which has an en suite. There is a double bed so tightly packed against three walls that there are hair-oil stains on the pillow end wall, and a variety of footmarks on the one opposite. I can see the footmarks belong to at least three different people, two of them women, with one set improbably high up the wall – possible evidence of sex with a yoga teacher or contortionist? Should I try to scrub the footmarks or leave them as evidence for the next guest to grace the bed? I decide to scrub one lot away, leaving the higher ones, because they impress me.

Then it is the en suite with its badly fitted shower door. The in-a-hurry guy hands me a squeegee, and shows me how to make an S shape to get all the soap lines off. With just a light press of the squeegee to the inside door, it breaks off its hinges and is about to topple over me. I am all John McEnroe: *This Can Not Be Happening Again*. Where is the fucking umpire of cleaning jobs? It is a heavy thing and, as I try to manipulate it back onto its hinges, I fall backwards, hitting the lever that turns the shower on. So I am pinioned against the shower wall, with the shower on, praying that I can at least get the door back to where it should be. OK, wait, if anyone comes in, I can say I am trying to see the shower, from the showerer's point of view, like they said in the agency. Looking for hairs. Except I am taking it one step further and actually using the shower. With all my clothes on. Unfortunately, this job is supervised not by the more forgiving hungover night worker, but by the testy, impatient guy anxious to get to his job for eight. I manage to get the shower off and lean the shower door against the tiled wall. I find the guy and say, "Hey, I'm really sorry but the door came off its hinges," figuring he will say, "Oh, that always happens, don't worry," but he says, "So you broke the shower door…" Diplomatically, he does not mention I am soaking wet.

He points to his watch and says he has to be out of the flat, therefore so do I, by half past eight, and shouldn't I get on with the hoovering? With wet hands, I stick the Hoover plug into its socket, risking electrocution because, really, what else could go wrong? He peers at me as I hoover and at quarter past, he goes, "Right, we need to finish now…" and I say, "Oh, I am done." I press the button that makes the cord disappear back into the vacuum cleaner, wishing, for a moment, that I could disappear with it. This month, anyway, I do not think I am going to be in the running for Cleaner of the Month.

Chapter Six

In September 1980 I moved into a house with guys who ran an underground newspaper. I got a couple of cleaning jobs and another job caring for elderly people in their own homes. I was attracted to jobs in homes. If I could not be in my own home, somebody else's home was almost as good.

I also got a job as a coat-check girl in a punk club. If I started to feel agoraphobic, I just took more pills and hid behind all the leather jackets. With the right dose of pills and suppositories, I could appear calm, not fall down, and even string a few sentences together. I loved the punk club, the energy of the music, the heads bobbing up and down, the crazed dancing, which was not really dancing at all but throwing yourself into other people. Of course, I was in my little leather-coated closet, dancing with myself and a sea of empty jackets. People – drunk on booze, on the music, on the possibility of sex with someone they had just met or slammed into – would stuff dollar bills into my tip jar. More often than not, in the mayhem, people would lose their tickets and say, "Sorry I lost my ticket. My one is a black leather jacket with studs." All the jackets were black leather with studs, so I would just give them the one that they pointed to (which may or may not have been their own) and everyone left happy. Maybe not with the right coat, but happy enough to tip generously.

Once a French guy tried to check his passed-out, naked-from-the-waist-up girlfriend into the coat check. I told him that he needed to take her out for air, or give her water, or call an ambulance. He explained in broken English that she always did this and that he would be back to fetch her when the gig was over. I covered her top half with jackets, and she had a slight smile on her face and pulled one of the jackets right up to her chin. I noticed she was beautiful, drunk as anything. It occurred to me that this might be a good plan B in the future, if the anxiety got too bad. Just drink to the point of passing out and get yourself checked into the coat check – to be fetched when the night was over. About every half hour or so, I would kneel down and whisper loudly into her ear, "Are you OK?" and she would smile slightly and say, "*Ah, oui.*" And sure enough at the end of the night the French guy came back, with another impossibly beautiful girl in tow. I said, "Do you want the one you came with as well?"

I enjoyed the voyeuristic qualities of working in the coat check. You checked the coats and watched havoc unfold around you. I liked walking back to my shared flat at two am and counting all the quarters I had made in tips. The flat itself was messy, but contained in its mess. We all had our own little systems of chaos. My room, the only single, was a mattress on the floor, covered in sheets and sometimes blankets. I had a clock radio by my bed and a sea of books and newspapers all within reach. We used to congregate in the living room and watch three televisions stacked up on each other. One had Benny Hill, one had sports and one was something like *Dallas*, or a daytime soap. Or we played records. Or one of my roommates would practise guitar. Usually two of us would sit at the kitchen table for morning coffee. We were quiet, but we were, in all senses, hanging out. They were guys and felt like older brothers to me. When one potential suitor started slipping letters of poetry under our door, addressed to me, I used to read the poetry aloud and we would all critique it. One of my roommates said, "Do you like this guy? You falling for this stuff?"

"Nah, I don't even understand it, and it doesn't even rhyme."

"We could beat him up if you want…"

"No, that's OK. It seems sort of mean… There's no harm, he's just a bad writer; plus, I don't like him in that way…"

He nodded and said, "Good answer." I felt a rush of love for him, and the other one. These guys had my back. We were messy, but it was our mess, our little made-up family. Me and my made-up accent and personality.

While I was working in the nightclub, I enrolled in a teacher training college. My thinking was, if I went into a blind panic, I could just set the kids some reading or a test and while they were all looking down at their papers, I would fish for the necessary pills and swallow them to get me through the rest of the day. I didn't feel any great calling to teach. It just struck me as something I could get away with. Buzzy had wanted me to be a teacher, thinking it a noble profession, but I thought, stupidly, that it was something that did not require a whole lot of smarts. You only ever had to be one page ahead of the kids in the workbook. Things like personality and behavioural issues were not on my radar. It was one of those jobs, surely, where I could continue doing drugs, and look like I had some degree of authority, merely by being bigger, physically, than my charges.

I had had at least one teacher when I was at school who was a full-blown lush. Lovely man, but nearly always just the right side of functioning, pissed. If he could get away with it, so could I, or so I thought. It was probably the most short-sighted vision I ever acted upon. Kids, as I was to discover, notice the slightest nuances in change of behaviour. If you are scared to death and think you are hiding it, you are never really hiding it from a kid.

In teacher training, I had to be this entirely other person. Entirely different from the person I was pretending to be in the first place. I dressed in corduroy suits and turtleneck sweaters, formal but friendly. I made lesson plans that were grandiose and impossible to implement with a group of rowdy ten-year-olds. "Today, class, you are all going to be planets in the solar system." Everybody wanted to be the sun. No one wanted to revolve. One girl was so disgusted with my lesson she stuck her fingers down her throat and registered her disapproval by throwing up all over my worksheet.

It was also a time in the Boston school system when primary schools were laying off physical education teachers, so that normal teachers had to learn how to teach PE. This proved to be a challenge. I had no hand-eye coordination, strength or speed, and the little I did have, the drugs took away. I would take the kids out into the yard, throw a ball at them and say, "Do your thing. That playing thing." And they would stand sullenly in a circle and tell me I had to tell them what the game was. I always chose dodgeball, a game I'd hated in school myself, but had no problem inflicting on this group. I was still getting panic attacks and, though I always made it to the primary school, I had trouble sitting in the lesson for theory. I found myself sitting by the door, making hasty exits, trying to find a cab I could not afford. I took more drugs, but not so much as to make my chalkboard writing shaky.

About three quarters of the way through my course, my mother called from Liverpool and told me my grandfather was dying and asked if I could come over as soon as possible. So, dosed up on a plethora of pharmaceuticals, I got myself to Liverpool and found my grandfather breathing noisily, gaspingly, in his giant bed. My mother and a nurse friend, Mae, were by his side. The nurse said to me, "You'll be gasping for a cuppa," and I said no, he was the gasping one, we'd do tea later.

He died a few hours after I got there. His chest had been rising and falling violently, rattling with fluid. Now and then he would stop breathing and Mae would take his pulse and shake her head as if to say, not quite yet, and then his chest would bellow out again. At some point during all these false endings, there was the real one, and he died, and to my eyes, it wasn't all that bad. He was in his own bed, he wasn't aware of anything, and if he was in any pain, which he probably was, it was over now. Mae told me to ring the hospital and tell them Mr Gould had just died, and would they send for the doctor to declare him dead, and then they would send someone to fetch the corpse. I rang and did as she said, and as I put the phone down, the door bell went. It was a man carrying a doctor's black bag. I said, "Wow, that was fast," and then, "He's up the stairs, turn right on the landing."

He went upstairs and then came down, pale, shaken. He said, "He's... well, he's dead."

And I said, "I know. That's why you're here."

He said, "I think there's been a mistake. I'm the chiropodist."

I burst out laughing and said, "I'm sorry, I thought you were the man who declares him dead. I mean, you did, but not officially."

He still looked bad, so I went and got us both some Scotch from my grandfather's stash, which he rarely touched and now would never touch again. Later on, a doctor came, and I remember this bit so well, better than all the other bits. He was small and very tidy and smelled of sandalwood soap, a scent I like the best. He asked who needed "Walium", for he couldn't say his Vs very well. I just remember holding out my hand. It was like getting communion, not that I had ever had communion, but it felt solemn and like a sort of ritual. I didn't even need water. I just knocked it to the back of my throat and later went to chase it with a little more Scotch. I have a great memory for doctors. I remember doctors better than most people remember lovers. I know how many I had, who gave me what, and who didn't.

Cleaning, London 2015
THE ILL WOMAN

THERE IS THE COUPLE WHERE the wife has a degenerative illness and the husband is the carer. They are hoarders – of
health-food supplements, clothes still in their shopping bags,
and carrier bags and boxes just full of stuff. The bed is flush
to a black-with-damp wall. The first thing I do is move the
bed away from the wall to try to scrub off the damp, and
this move reveals porno mags crammed into blue carrier
bags. There are things, during cleaning jobs, that you have
to "unsee" but, as the couple are in the basement and I am
on the ground floor, I figure it is OK to look. I don't know
much about porn but this looks like the soft stuff. Mainly
short, curvy women with balloon lips and gigantic tits. There
is one with a woman with the most freakishly enormous
knockers on the cover, and I rub my back, imagining how
much she must hurt, having to lug those torpedoes everywhere.

This makes me think of the time when my mother was
a receptionist for a tit magazine called *Jugs*, in NY in the
early 80s. They thought my mother's English accent made
her sound more classy. She told me then, "It is a terrible
thing to have to answer the phone saying, 'Jugs!' in a perky
voice, all day long." I love this memory, and I stare at the tit
mag, thinking about my mother. The husband walks past the

bedroom and sees me staring at it, and my first impulse is to blurt out "It's not what you think! I'm smiling at your porn because I am thinking about my mother!" And I realise this is probably the worst thing to say, so I just say brightly, "I've seen bigger ones, in the *Sun*" to let him know that I am OK with his tit mags, and this is our secret, and it's no big deal. He pretends not to hear (or see) and scuttles past to tend to his wife.

She has the sort of tubercular cough I have heard in medical soap operas, where the doctor gets his stethoscope and says, "I don't like the sound of this." She calls for him, when she is in the bathroom, when she is trying to get from one part of the house to another. And he goes to her, and they murmur to each other and he says encouraging things like: "That's it... nearly there, love." There is a tenderness there that hurts me.

On the second clean, they have to leave me in the house while they go to the hospital, and he tells me some workmen will be coming to finish installing a wheelchair lift which goes from the bottom level of the garden to the top one – will I let them in, and show them into the garden? This is all fine. I let the guys in, they go out to the muddy garden, and I say in a voice not at all my own, but a sort of mumsy, mockney, "Now don't you go treading all that mud into my noice clean kitchen, lads." They fiddle with the lift, I mop the floors, and it is all wonderfully uneventful until one of the guys asks if I will give the lift a trial run, so I can sign off the paperwork and they can leave.

I blanch. I don't want the responsibility. What if it is fine when I use it and then gets stuck when she does? All this, plus it is raining. I just don't want to do it.

"I have nothing to do with them," I say. "I am just the cleaner. If it's in any way technical I will probably forget the instructions."

"No, really," the guy replies, "it takes no brains whatsoever to operate it. Red button for stop, green button for go."

We stand on the lift, in the rain, and I press the green button. Some sort of revving noise starts up and the lift begins to take off, but then stops midway, where you can see a mid-section of cut-out earth and stones, as in a picture in a secondary school geology text. The man presses the green button again, and then the red button, and hops off the lift to examine the undercarriage. "Ah, there's a branch caught up in it," he tells me. "See, that's the magic. If anything is wrong, it stops."

"Yeah, but what is she supposed to do, if she is in the wheelchair?" I say. "She can't just hop off and remove the branch."

"No, her carer will do that."

I picture her venturing out alone one day, in the lift, and the thing stopping. She will be in the chair, waiting for someone to come, caught between the lower and upper garden. Her husband will come in from his errand to the chemist or natural health-food shop and find her on the lift, midway between the underground and the overground, hovering between life and burial.

Chapter Seven

In Boston, in the early 80s, I had a nice psychiatrist, who was very generous with the old prescription pad but felt that one of the roots of my problem, particularly my problem with swallowing, which translated to a problem with eating, was to do with a phobia of vomiting. Vomiting, a very messy business, the opposite of cleaning – though the people who purge on purpose would probably say that it is very cleansing. Your insides literally coming out for all the world to see, if you don't make it somewhere private in time. It is all the smelly, semi-digested ugliness inside you, coming outside you, forcibly. I just can't stand it and never could. I have since learned that this is a very common phobia, but back then, it was not one of the popular ones. My therapist was experimenting with a technique called gradual exposure. This involved first looking at a picture of someone being sick until it no longer frightened me. To me, the picture looked too posed. A pretty girl wrapped around a toilet, her hair and make-up perfect. The next thing he did was hire a copy of the film *An Unmarried Woman*, in which Jill Clayburgh throws up into a bin in New York City. It was very hard for me to watch. He kept pausing it at the bit where she chucked up. I tried to imagine what it would be like, meeting her at a party: "Wow, Jill, I've seen you throw up hundreds of times!"

The next step was to get a little container of vomit that I had to open and look at and just sort of keep it around, until it no longer bothered me. He told me he'd been able to get the vomit as a doctor working in a hospital. It may or may not have been real sick. It may have been sweet-corn and tomatoes and Parmesan cheese and milk, but it seemed to be the real thing to me. At first, I shrank from it as if it were a monster. At the time, I trusted his instincts, backed up by medical journal studies. I remember putting the little Tupperware bowl of sick, which was double-bagged in case it leaked, into my bag, as if it were the most normal thing in the world to do. It jostled for room next to all my pills and potions, this container of some-one else's insides, supposedly, which now I had to carry around with me, like a pet toy poodle.

My new boyfriend was an artist and he had got used to my peculiar ways and phobias. We shared my single, unmade mattress on the floor, and once, going through some papers on my desk, he found my little tub of sick. He asked what it was. I told him it was vomit, but not mine. The strangeness of this explanation only strikes me now, as I write this. At the time I think I said it in a very offhand way, "Oh, just a tub of sick." I told him it was a sort of project, and that with him being an artist, he should respect it, even if it was disgusting.

"This is a joke, right?"

I told him it was not a joke and that I was crazy, and it might be better if we were not boyfriend and girlfriend any more. I was a great one for the "It's not you, it's me" line because it was always the truth. I had too many weird little secrets.

Still, we rallied. We took a trip to the mountains and went hiking. He got a headache and I fished around my giant rucksack of drugs and pulled out a random pill. I don't know what I gave him, but it made him all drowsy and floppy. At one point in the night I said, "You have to un-flop – I think there's a bear outside the tent." And he said, "Whatever, tell it to go away." This was one pill of the sort I took handfuls of daily, and he was at least twice my size. I realised I was developing a great tolerance for drugs. I had literally climbed a mountain on drugs, with cantaloupes in my rucksack because it had not occurred to me to pack lightly, only to pack food that I really liked.

The next morning, over lukewarm coffee heated over a campfire, I told him we – or our remains – could have been found on the mountain, having been eaten by the bear. And he said, "If the bear had eaten you, he would have been so drugged up he would have forgotten what he was eating in the middle and just dozed off. You would probably just have to have an arm bitten off or something."

We broke up but stayed friends and I carried on with all my stupid jobs and drugs and going to the shrink. Eventually the shrink said that the only way to get over the phobia was to actually be sick. This was the logical conclusion to the gradual exposure, to do the thing you fear the most. He was sure I would get over the phobia if I could experience what a short, small deal it was. He had read that a safe way to do it was to drink a lot of salt water, loads, and then nature would just take its course. When the day came, I cried my eyes out and started to drink glasses and glasses of salty water. Nothing happened. He told me to drink more and then stick my fingers down my throat. I did this and gagged a bit but nothing else happened. I felt terribly sick but could not be sick. Our time was up, the experiment had failed, and I decided then and there that really the only way to live life was to ask for as many drugs as possible and take them as regularly as possible.

Pharmaceutically functioning, I managed to finish my teacher training course and get myself a job as an assistant teacher in a private school in New York City. The school was very liberal. The teachers were called by their first names, the class sizes were small, and the class I was placed in, for four- and five-year-olds, mainly got to "learn through play". The pay was appalling, so I had to supplement my income by working at the afterschool club, where kids had healthy snacks and played inside or out, depending on the weather.

At first, I enjoyed the chaos, the happy wildness of the kids. There was less about health and safety in those days, so we had a wood-working table, and five-year-olds would hammer and saw as I milled around the room, making sure everyone was happy and busy. We had a pet we were told was a praying mantis, a rare insect, which one kid killed by feeding it the remains of a McDonald's. The insect was called Cyndi Lauper and we buried it in Washington Square Park, with each child allowed to express in a eulogy what they liked best about Cyndi. We sang "Girls Just Wanna Have Fun" and put her in the ground. It was probably the least traumatic funeral I've ever been to.

What I was finding out, the hard way, was that I did not like teaching. I was not a natural. I was not interested in watching kids colour, or build blocks, or make very bad birdhouses. After lunch, they would bring out these yoga mats and have a rest, while the main teacher and I did paperwork and she would put on a Vivaldi record, to calm them down. When she was off sick or having a break, I would change the record to the New York Dolls or the Ramones and the kids would spring from their mats, going mental, jumping up and down, racing around the room. I told myself this was good, I was wearing them out, the parents would thank me. But it doesn't really work like that. You get a kid all fired up and they stay that way, hyper, until they melt down and cry or say they've got a bellyache. One time, as the kids zipped round the room, and the primary teacher came back to see the chaos I was encouraging, I knew it was time for a career rethink. I was not asked back for another term.

That summer I worked at a temp agency for office work. One company put me on switchboard after I lied and said I'd had plenty of experience. After disconnecting every call I got, the office manager took me off switchboard and told me I had to run errands. She put a hugely heavy franking machine in my hand and told me to go over to the big post office and get the money on it topped up, and then come back and do a mailout. This seemed

OK. I could take my time going to the post office, I could look at the wanted criminal poster there, and just enjoy the summer sunshine. I was daydreaming about this, until she clapped her hands and said, "Don't mess this up, and do it quickly. Run. Run like a bunny."

There are certain phrases that stick with you for life. "Run like a bunny" is one of them. Did bunnies run? Surely they hopped. This girl, she had the big shoulder pads, she had a clipboard, she had a librarian's bun and fake eyebrows, she drank a slimming shake for lunch – she was not my kind of girl.

"Run like a bunny?" I asked.

"YES! YOU SHOULD HAVE BEEN GONE LIKE FIVE MINUTES AGO! FAST! NOW!"

I looked her squarely in the eyes and muttered, "I will run like a bunny," and then I put the franking machine down and hopped towards the elevator. She bellowed, "That's SO not funny. You are SO fired!"

That evening during rush hour, I agreed to meet my mother on the steps of the NYC library, where all those years before I'd read about the death of my father. I saw her and said, "I was just fired today," and she said, "So was I!" and we embraced and laughed. They had sacked her from *Jugs* for occasionally bursting into helpless giggles after saying "Jugs!" to strangers on the phone. There we were, on the steps where I was once so sad, laughing our heads off at our unemployability, and her inability to say "Jugs" with the necessary gravitas.

Next, I applied for a job as a substitute teacher in Brooklyn. This was the worst job of my life. The only requirements for it were to pass a basic English test and to be fingerprinted. I got a job teaching a first-grade class, one whose pupils had been streamed for behavioural problems. There were 35 children in one class. I did not have enough desks. I did not have an assistant. Most of the kids could neither read nor write their own name. They were meant to be about seven years old, but I had some in there as old as nine or ten, because if you didn't pass the test to get out of first grade, they made you repeat it the next year.

I looked very young for my age, and repeatedly had kids from the older classes stopping by my door and asking, "Yo, Ms Kirsch, you be sixteen?" and I said no, and they shook their heads in disbelief before abandoning me to six hours of sheer chaos. One of the kids just ran around the room in circles all day. They brought in knives from home. They had packed lunches of soda pop and candy bars, which made the hyper ones more hyper, and the quiet ones zonk out in these sort of sugar-rush come-down comas. I was out of my depth. I could never get them settled down enough to even begin to learn.

I used to ride the subway home shaking, until one day I took the train to the Lower East Side. I knew on certain streets, in certain doorways, the junkies would sell you their Valium scrips or pills. I did another two months of this job, on enough Valium to keep me sedated without actually falling asleep at the desk.

I left that job for the relative ease of reception work in a creative design agency. The phone rarely rang. My job was to creatively make the petty cash receipts look like valid business expenses, and answer the phone "brightly". I didn't even have to say "Jugs", just the name of the agency. One day, one of the designers said to me, "A client has told me that when you answer the phone, you don't give out the right image. You sound like you are clinically depressed. We are sparkly, upbeat. Frankly, you sound really down, or as if you're on drugs. Can you work on that?"

I said I would, and I started to answer the phone in the personality of a coked-up quiz show host. A few weeks later, just before Christmas, they fired me. They said, "It just isn't working out."

I said I understood. But really, the main thing I understood was that there was some game you had to play to be a grown-up and I didn't know how to play it convincingly. I just knew that when I was on drugs, I didn't much care. With the complexities of the American health care system, it was hard to get a doctor if you didn't have a job. I was running out of drugs. You know those old films that show the passage of time with months dropping off a calendar? I see the months of my life dropping away in a similar fashion with scrip sheets, most of them written legitimately, some written insanely, by myself in a facsimile of the tired doctor with bad handwriting. One badly thought-out ruse was getting my optician nurse flatmate in Brooklyn to nick a scrip sheet for me from her job. It never occurred to me that an optician would have very little reason to write out a scrip sheet for 150 Valium. How nervous could eyes get? I went to a multi-purpose drugstore in Spanish Harlem, which also sold toy guns, possibly real ones, and candy and strangely, mounds of incontinence products, and handed over my fake scrip. The assistant said something in Spanish to the pharmacist, who told me, in unnaturally formal English, that in cases like this, it was customary to call the prescribing doctor to check that everything was correct. I panicked and ran out of the shop, the only visible white girl running madly towards the subway in Spanish Harlem. Puerto Rican boys on stoops, sipping from brown bags, pointed and said, "*Mira, mira, loca chica blanca*" ("Look. Crazy white girl").

The backlash fell hard and fast. My flatmate got in trouble. Nearly fired, but for the fact that she lied and said I had come to visit her and stole the sheet myself. She also told me there was an investigation pending from the Drug Enforcement Agency. It seemed like a good time to quit my job and move.

Cleaning, London 2015
THE DRUG DEALER

A TWO-BEDROOM FLAT IN WHITECHAPEL. When I arrive at the flat, the guy who answers the door says vaguely, "Just do whatever, except, don't touch anything that looks, um, just don't touch anything in my room. I mean you can pick it up to dust or whatever. I have some important things."

This foxes me. What, in a person's flat, qualifies as important? Surely this is a subjective thing. And, as I start to ask, his phone goes off and he picks it up and soon begins a heated conversation about money. "No more credit, man, you owe me at least 600. No, man, no, don't call unless you have the dosh. Yeah… safe. Byeeeee!"

I'm struck by the malevolent tone of the first bit of the conversation, followed by the girly-fashion-PR "Byeeee!"

He goes out but not before gesturing to where his cleaning stuff is. There is a bucket, some washing-up liquid and lots of bicarbonate of soda.

The first bedroom is immaculate, a hotel-style Degas print on the wall, *The Da Vinci Code* on the bedside table and about 30 pairs of boxed, seemingly never-worn trainers lined up against one of the walls. The second bedroom is a biohazard, full of newspapers, tin foil, half-eaten takeaways and dirty laundry. On the window side of the bed are hundreds of metallic mini-canisters, the sort I see littering the streets of Shoreditch. There are also cellophane packets of what looks like weed and several pharmaceutical-looking boxes with Indian writing on them. Bingo. The guy is a drug dealer. I can't decide if I am impressed or appalled that he makes no attempt to hide his stash. I love that he does not know that my cleaning his room is fraught with risk, that I will nick the drugs, or ring the cops, or nick the ones I like and then ring the cops. The fact that I am thinking about taking the drugs at all means that my recovery from drug addiction is not going well.

I am, at this point, what they call a "dry drunk". Not drinking or using, but still obsessed with the thought of using, of drinking, of, at this particular clean, being a kid in a sweetie shop. I am doing OK, mopping, dusting, polishing, throwing stuff out, sorting dirty clothes from clean, when, reaching underneath the bed to rescue a stray pair of socks, I find a box of American Xanax, a drug I was prescribed many times while I was in the US, a drug that is a familiar, reliable friend.

It never occurs to me to steal. What does occur to me is to wait until he comes back and make some sort of ongoing arrangement, where I clean, and he pays me in Xanax. For a moment, I seem able to forget that I have lost everyone and everything I held dear through my drug addiction. I live alone and clean houses because it is all I can really do right now. I back out of the room, as if it were booby-trapped. I take one long glance back, as if looking at a lover I will never see again.

Chapter Eight

A few weeks before my final month's rent ran out, I went to visit Buzzy. It had been a couple of years since I had seen him, and I was told by a friend that he was staying in the Jane West Hotel. It's where you stayed if you didn't have much money. It had been, in the olden days, a place for decrepit sailors, and also the place, so the junkies who lived there liked to tell me, where they put the survivors of the Titanic. Just as I was about to make my way down there, the friend, who worked for another downtown magazine, rang me back and told me the Jane West story was just a cover story, and that Buzz was in reduced circumstances and living in a storage facility. If he couldn't even afford the Jane West, Buzz was for sure down on his luck. On the other hand, it was a storage facility in the West Village, so that was OK. Buzz had long given up on newspapers and was now driving a taxi, I guess not making enough money to pay rent for anywhere.

The storage space technically belonged to Andy Warhol, or at least the company that ran Warhol's *Interview* magazine, because this was where all the unsold copies of *Interview* were stored. Buzz opened the door just a crack, his eyes hovering over the chain lock. Once he saw it was me, he closed the door and went through a long process of unlocking all the locks.

Inside was a revelation, a little room with all the furniture built with back issues of *Interview* magazine. "Jesus, Buzz, where do you sleep?"

"With Brooke Shields. I mean, the Brooke Shields issue." Sure enough, there was a thin piece of foam covering a whole bed-shaped stack of Brooke Shields.

"Warhol would LOVE this!" I marvelled at his papier mâché skills, though he seemed to skip the flour and water glue bit and just stack the magazines up to build whatever it was he needed: a bed, a chair, a table, even a commode, which was an assemblage of a broken chair, a bin bag and shredded magazines.

"But Warhol will never know, or I will get evicted," he said, letting me know, in no uncertain terms, that this arrangement had to remain top secret.

We soon got down to the main purpose of my visit, which was to seek advice from this fatherly figure I had come to respect and admire, more so now for his ingenuity at living in a storage shed.

"I need advice. I did a stupid thing and it's probably best that I leave NY for a while."

I told him the story of the optician and the forged scrip and the DEA, and the part of the story that upset him most was the part that upset me the most, which is that I didn't actually get the drugs.

This man, this giver of bad career advice, thought that I just might stay in New York if I met the right guy. I told him it was not likely I was going to fall in love before my rent ran out and I was served… whatever papers the DEA serve to people who have committed minor forgeries, if they follow that sort of thing up.

Even though he had told me to be a teacher, and I had become a teacher, and hated it, I trusted him implicitly. With his handsome face, chiselled and smart, his funeral parlour suits, his quiet seriousness, he had me hanging on his every word. The fact that he spoke in such a quiet voice – barely a whisper, made me lean in to listen, which made everything he said seem more ominous and important than it was. When I think back to those times, I can see the volume control was set to low because he was not supposed to be there. That, and his vocal chords were muted by smoking dope and munching Valium.

New York was getting uglier. This much we jointly established. The poor were getting poorer, and rents were skyrocketing. We convened in the room of magazines, discussing our exit strategies while taking pills, as he reclined on Brooke Shields, and I sat in a chair made up of Tom Cruises.

I was going to England in a few weeks, unless of course I fell in love with a good man. Buzz felt this was possible. He persisted with the idea that I should go on more dates with boys. I might meet "the one" and change my mind.

I did try and take his advice about going on more dates before I left New York. Two guys, two "dates". The first guy showed up at my apartment about two hours late. I thought we could walk around Brooklyn, get some pizza at one of the late-night joints and then I would tell him

I was leaving and um, bye, and stuff. But he wound up being weird, and I decided to out-weird him, on a sort of weirdathon. I just could not let him be weirder than I was.

He rang the bell and when I buzzed him in, he walked very slowly and heavily up the stairs, one foot tread way heavier than the other. I thought his footfall sounded like a zombie's, and I was not that far off the mark, because when he arrived at the door, he had blood pouring from his mouth. I said, "Oh my God, what happened, did you get beaten up?" You know, your usual first-date opening line. And he grinned, dripping blood everywhere, and said, "I'm not, like, actually bleeding. I just thought it would be fun to look like I was." He explained, blood dripping from his gob, that he was an extra on a student film shoot, and they paid him in free blood capsules. He walked in, leaving a trail of fake blood. I rushed into the bathroom, took a toilet roll and started mopping up after him. I said, "Wow, this is fun," and he laughed and said, "I thought you would like it."

"You got any more?" I asked. "Do they taste bad? If you accidentally swallow one, will you be poisoned and possibly start to bleed for real?"

"Do you want one?"

I said I would have all five. This was, I would later find out, in a rehab in Bournemouth, typical addict behaviour. Why have one when you could have five? I took the five and stuffed them in my mouth and started to fake-bleed in large amounts. At which point, one of my roommates walked in. She took in the scene and said, "Oh my fucking God, did that guy beat you up?"

"No, it's fake blood. He got it from a video shoot. He thought it would be funny, so he gave me some too, but actually now I can see I am bleeding over everything, and we've nearly run out of toilet roll."

She said, "When are you actually moving out? The actual date?"

A few nights later, when I was packing, the second date called. Buzz had set this one up. I said I was sorry, I couldn't go out, but he could come over and help me pack and in exchange I would get us beer and pizza. He said that sounded OK. Not that exciting but actually he'd heard my part of Brooklyn did pretty good pizza.

The guy came over. He was very good-looking. He was a journalist, who'd just gone from a weekly paper to a big national one. He was nice, he was attractive, he had a good job, and now he was in my front room in Brooklyn, watching me pack.

After about an hour, he said, "Is this the date?"

"This is the date."

I asked him to come downstairs and help me put my stuff in the cab. We said goodbye and I thanked him for being such a good sport. He said nothing but smiled quizzically, and I went to Queens in a cigarette fog, shoving Compazine up my bum in the back of the cab.

I woke up late, in the same bed I slept in as a child. I wrote long, crazy letters to friends and ex-boyfriends I had left in Boston. I was 24. I had been to a good school, a not-so-good college and had been on and off prescription drugs most of my post-father life. None of this struck me as odd or dysfunctional. I blamed all my problems on

America in general, New York in particular.

As usual I had no plan other than to leave the place I was in. In between countries and boyfriends, and somewhere between living and not really living. In between. But that's life on drugs all over, in between consciousness and self-induced coma.

Cleaning, London 2016
IN BETWEEN JOBS

IT IS NOT OFTEN I clean for people out of work or between jobs. It's one of the hardest things for people to justify, not cleaning your own home if you are at home much of the day. This is an actor in between jobs, his partner clearly supporting, for the time being, the both of them. His face looks sort of familiar, a character actor. A criminal on *The Bill*. The father of a gunshot victim in *Casualty*. He is polite, tells me what needs to be done, but is clearly inconvenienced by the back injury of their regular cleaner, their treasure. People still say "treasure". Like they say, "my rock" with the praise of the "damning-with-faint" variety.

As I dust dust-free shelves and mop an immaculate floor, I hear him answer the phone, loudly, gaily, his speech punctuated by "no problemo" and "absolutely". A tone that suggests enthusiasm but actually smacks of desperation. I know that tone. I've employed it myself in periods of unemployment. He scours the trade papers and keeps going outside to smoke. I'm pressing his shirts, the tip of the iron releasing the impenetrable and seemingly detergent-proof whiff of the underarms, but I do not have the nerve to ask if he is sure these shirts are from the clean pile rather than the dirty one. I cannot work out their system. I bet the Treasure knows his shirts.

I can tell my presence irritates him.

When I need to mop the area where he is sitting, he gamely gets up and goes into the other room. Then, when I have to mop that room, he goes back to where he was sitting, tiptoeing over the wet floor. There is a look of irritated embarrassment and unjustified raised hackles, all in the curve of his arched eyebrows. We don't speak to each other. We just make faces. This guy is a bloody good actor, conveying all the quiet rage of being mopped out of his own flat, the lines on his forehead suggesting that he is sorry for stepping on a mopped floor, only NOT really sorry because it's his own floor, hardwood, cost a small fortune. I stare at his face too much. He knows that I know him from somewhere. I want to say, "Hey, I'd hire you. You have a very expressive upper quadrant of face. If I were giving you a review, it would be a rave. You could play an out-of-work actor!"

A few weeks later I check the agency website and see that he has given me a mediocre review, which is fair, because I didn't do as good a job as their Treasure. But I feel injured, because I would have given him a great review. It looks like I am not going to be Cleaner of the Month this month, either.

Chapter Nine

"You are pretty well travelled for an agoraphobic," said my friend Julie, who came to meet me off the train at Euston. I had gone to stay with my aunt in Liverpool for a few months and came down to London with the notion of writing for a music newspaper. Julie was right. For an agoraphobic, I did seem to get around a fair bit, but I was an agoraphobic on drugs, and these drugs gave me the confidence to stray beyond the proverbial garden walls that hemmed in all the other agoraphobics I read about in magazine articles. I still carried a self-help for agoraphobia book around, for good measure. It was by the queen of the genre, Claire Weekes. The book was written well before the medical community decided Valium was a bad thing, so Claire's advice was, do try to go to the supermarket, and try to "float" above the anxiety, but if you cannot, just take a Valium. As I could never grasp the concept of floating, I just did the Valium bit instead, and wound up, after a hiatus in Liverpool with my auntie, in London, with a half-baked plan to stay with a friend's ex-boyfriend until I found my own little bedsit, or met a guy I could live with, whichever came first.

The guy who took me on as a lodger was a struggling actor who was also a lorry driver. During our first conversation, I learned he had been in a film, that he thought Gorbachev was the bee's knees and would save the world, that he was a communist, and that if he lived in a communist country he could probably be an actor full time. I could tell, with all the Soviet love he was giving off, that he was probably not a fan of the USA or people from it, but I had long since abandoned my fake English accent and so there seemed to be a natural animosity and begrudging feeling that he was just doing me a favour, like, for 20 quid a week. And what was my story, he wanted to know: why did I leave the USA? What could I say to get him on side? That it was not as good as the USSR? That I was trying to travel my way out of a natural disposition to agoraphobia? I opted for the truth.

"I am under investigation by the Drug Enforcement Administration for forging a prescription for an improbably large amount of Valium."

He shook his head, bewildered. "You are very... open."

"Well, I guess," I said, nervously, not sure if this were a compliment or an insult.

He said, "I mean, it's so very bloody AMERICAN!"

"The being open bit or the Valium bit?"

"Both!"

This was March, and very cold and damp, more so in the flat than outside of it, and he told me a great lie. He said that if the gas metre starts to approach the zero mark, the pilot light goes out but the gas is still released, which will mean the flat will fill up with gas and if I strike a match we will all go up in flames. I should feed the metre with 50-pence pieces as often as possible, and so avoid the combustion scenario.

Though I had started freelancing for a music paper, my income was patchy at best, non-existent at worst. The only way to stay warm was to wear my overcoat all the time, and eat Readybrek for breakfast, lunch and dinner, for it was cheap, hot and filling. I was not long in that flat before the lorry driver told me that I must go. He offered no explanation except to say, "I think you know why..." but I didn't. I also didn't care.

I sofa-surfed for a while and finally found a bedsit in Hackney. It was a basement – huge, and very cheap. The landlord told me that occasionally his grandson came to stay in a different part of the basement but he wouldn't disturb me. This was only partially true. He would come and go and leave his hypodermics on top of my kitchenette cupboards. How weird it is to me now that I drew such a large moral distinction between his heroin addiction and my growing dependence on prescription tranquillisers, if and when I could get them. Plus, I would never be that careless. I always hid my stash and, apart from answering the odd emergency plea, never, ever shared it.

The bedsit was grim, and damp, but, apart from occasional visits from the heroin addict, it was private. I went to Ridley Road Market and bought a roll of colourful African fabric and threw sheets of it all over the damp furniture. It has occurred to me that my throw solution to beat-up furniture, which has carried on to my present day flat, is the decorative equivalent of drugs. Just throw something over it – your sofa, your brain – and no one will know how shit scared you are, how shabby you are. Throw dry stuff over the damp stuff. It will get damp ,too, but it buys you a few days of respectable living, in a cheap-tat sort of way.

Cleaning, London 2015
RISING DAMP

THE CLIENT IS AN INDEPENDENT radio producer, really nice, polite, helpful when his Hoover keeps clogging up or not spinning. This clean evokes broken dreams. Not the flat itself, which is riddled with rising damp, one half of it being on basement level – it brings to mind the novelty song "I'm just a mole and I live in hole". But the fact that this guy is a happy mole. He has a great dog and a great job. The bit that depresses me is that I was once on the radio, for a short spell. I loved it more than any other job I ever did. Eventually a position came up as a trainee radio producer. My job interview for that position went so very badly wrong that I have panic attacks thinking about it. The panel asked how I would "lighten up" my proposed radio programme about heroin addicts on needle exchange programmes – this was not to stop addiction, but to try to prevent AIDS. I said I would cut to the Velvet Undergound song "Heroin". The suggestion was met with blank stares, and not only did I not get the trainee position, but I never worked in radio again. All this shame revisits me while I clean the flat of the successful radio producer.

He is often at home during the clean, editing a bit of a story. Just going over one line over and over again, hearing something not quite right that I cannot hear myself.

I always feel a great well of sadness when I clean this flat. It occurs to me at one point that it will never look very much better without some major work – damp coursing, a paint job, new furniture, a new kitchen, but that is not the bit that depresses me. He has a lot of the same books as I do. He is doing a job I would love to do myself. He is in his little office, with his dog, while I am in the bathroom next door, removing mushrooms from the floor tiles with a knife and some bleach. He is doing what he loves, or seems to love. I am doing what I have to do because in my drinking and drugging years, I de-skilled myself out of the market.

It is the first job in which I blame my tools. The Hoover does not suck up damp dog hair. I scrape and bleach the mushroom mould but it will be back the next week. He is blissfully oblivious, entrenched in his next radio feature. In time, he approaches me about being an interviewee for a programme he is making about what is known as the "sharing economy", where everyone benefits from services being provided. I am glad to participate, glad to be part of radio in any form. He asks me about my cleaning day, and I can't remember if I do or don't tell him that for the first clean, I get only two quid. Either way, he leaves it out. That not everyone gets an equal share of the sharing economy.

Chapter Ten

I got a job in a bagel bakery and my boss was called Moses. He said to me, "Are you Jewish?" And I said yes. And then he asked me why I was not married and why I didn't have children. A cut-to-the-chase kind of biblically named guy. I took the job, and Moses kept trying to matchmake me, including on one occasion with the kid son his delivery driver. This was the second avuncular figure in my life who felt all my problems would be solved by meeting the right guy.

"So you are happy to be 25, unmarried and barren?" he said. I replied that I was delighted and liked nothing more than working in his shop.

"Ah, a career girl! This is OK for a while, but you would be much happier married, with children."

His words would come back to haunt me. He was theoretically right. In time, I would be married twice, the second time with children and divinely happy. But then I would fuck it all up, so he was a bit wrong, too.

I got married the first time, after a brief courtship, the day after storms tore up trees from the pavements in 1987. It was an omen I had ignored. Our courtship had been drink-fuelled on his side, speed-fuelled on mine. We were both journalists in the music business and none of this seemed abnormal or excessive. We just had different poisons and different comedowns from them. Everybody we knew drank and did drugs, to some extent. It was hard for me to gauge what could pass for normal consumption. But most people in the business, from what I could see, drank and did drugs for fun. It was when you had to do this stuff simply to feel normal that it became a problem. Where did that leave me? I had used drugs to feel normal from the get-go.

Speed is an unfortunate drug choice for an anxious person. I thought it would make time go more quickly. And in a way, it did, but the time that was flying was full of panic attacks and unspoken terrors, all of which could be undone by drinking more. For a short while, we managed just about OK. We played house. He went to a day job and I freelanced but he paid most of the bills. He was a gentleman with a razor-sharp wit, and there was a lot of laughter, and we seemed to like a lot of the same stuff. We shared music obsessions, playing the same records over and over again, following certain artists fanatically. You could get away with this in the name of research. All the normal lines of work life and home life, real friends and people who were nice to you to get publicity for their bands, were blurred. In our minds, we had a ton of friends and loads of free stuff: records, booze, lunches, trips. On the surface, even beyond the surface, I had nothing to complain about. I could not call him out on his sometimes excessive drinking while I was on the way to deviating my septum with harsh, cheap speed.

Not long into the marriage, I was sent to interview a shy American country singer for a magazine. I had interviewed lots of pop and country stars and was never particularly starstruck or nervous, but this guy was different. He had this real Southern gentleman charm, a soft-spoken, considered way of talking. He had a quality that was rare in the music business, in that he was unassuming. He spoke carefully, not giving too much away about his personal life. I had never had a crush on anyone I had interviewed, but this man turned my knees to jelly. He asked me if I wanted to go to dinner that night with him and his manager and I said yes. When we got to the restaurant, he ordered ice cream, so I did as well. I loved that: cutting to the innocent chase of ice cream, ignoring the starters and mains. When you are writing an article about someone who does not say very much, everything that happens takes on a meaning that is probably more a personal mental construct than anything actually significant. Plus once a crush starts to build up a head, everything means something it probably doesn't. Years before, when I was similarly infatuated with a devastatingly handsome slow talker in Boston, everything the guy said, which was not very much, in my mind was a metaphor for about 50 other things. A strong jawline and Roman nose made up for all the words unsaid. One night, when I was sobbing uncontrollably about him to a flatmate, she said, "I know this kind of guy, it's like he can finish your sentences." And I blew my nose, thought about it and said, "Actually he can barely finish his own, but it's there in his distant gazes."

This country singer was the same... a complete antidote to the rapid-fire puns and wit of my husband and speed-fuelled drivel that made up my own discourses.

I was still living with my husband at the time, but I wanted to escape. I could see he was falling out of love with me, quite rapidly. A few nights after meeting the country singer, I asked my husband, or rather said to him, "I don't think you love me any more." And he said no, he did not, and then I knew it was really over. I was sad, I had failed as a wife, or something, but maybe, just maybe, I could now be free for the country singer, if he could be free for me. Once again, I threw all my stuff in the back of a taxi, chain-smoking, and went to stay in a hotel for a few days, until another friend came to the rescue and found me a rented room in central London.

The room was tiny, a little former larder off the kitchen, and I knew I wouldn't last there.

But in the meanwhile, I covered my wall with pictures of the country singer and it was like being twelve again. Except I was 27: old enough to know the impossibility of any kind of relationship with this man, but immature enough to obsessively pore over his lyrics, looking for hidden meaning, and to fashion my hair in the same Eraserhead-era frizzy up-do. A crush was so much more fun than a relationship or marriage. I preferred pining for the unattainable to wandering down the supermarket aisles, trying to figure out what to make for dinner. And pining is a heady mixture of love and grief; you work the impossible object of your wack-job affection into every gap in the conversations you have, with those people you have not yet bored to death.

Strangely, despite all the upset and upheavals and uncertainty about how I was going to live, where I was going to live, how I was going to get over my obsession with the country singer, anxiety-wise I was having a good period. I have never been able to explain or understand these occasional periods of wellness, apart from with the theory that being struck down by a dumb crush – and there are probably smart crushes; I have just never had one – displaced the craving for narcotic oblivion. Had I studied them forensically, the good bits, the well bits, the unworried bits, I might have been able to recreate them without using drugs, and without manufacturing a crush. Maybe, or maybe not. I was just grateful when they came, which was not very often. I remember not being dependent on drugs for this period of two or three years, just drinking socially.

I thought, ah, all I have to do is live in chaos, and I won't be nervous. To some extent, this proved to be true. Still, it had to be a calculated chaos: I never wanted to find out what it felt like to be the left one. I wanted to do the leaving, always. In this case my husband beat me to it, verbally, but I left physically. I was getting to like these drama-queen, quick-taxi exits.

Cleaning, London 2015
SHE'S LEAVING HOME

YOU'D THINK THIS WAS A common enough scenario. Young love. Wild nights. Sex. Drugs. Careers. A deposit. An afford-able mortgage with two better-than-average incomes. Loving and rich parents on both sides who slip money into their joint account. Dinner parties: the food is nou-velle cuisine, tiny portions on large plates to accommo-date cocaine-diminished appetites. She gets pregnant in her early 30s, when she has climbed so far in her career she can take as much maternity leave as she wants. If they move just a little further out, they could get a bigger place, with a room for a nanny...

But I did only one clean where I guessed this to be the pre-leaving scenario. Victorian conversion, one house split into three very small two-bedroom flats. He opened the door in his pyjama bottoms and gestured me into the frankly filthy living-room. He made me instant coffee and said, unbidden, "I haven't really tidied since my wife left me."

I put on my sympathy face, but not for very long. I didn't actually want him to tell me the whole story. "So, you just need a general deep clean, is that right?"

He nodded and led me to a cupboard where the clean-ing stuff and coats were kept. There was one pink, fluffy jacket that smelled of ground-floor-department-store-mixed-sample perfumes. There was the latest-model, see-through vacuum cleaner. There was a plastic apron with fake tits on it. He took the apron off the hook and handed it to me. I shook my head and said, no thanks, I cleaned in my sweats and didn't need an apron.

He persisted, "I think you should wear it. It's funny."

"I think it's yours," I said diplomatically, "and funnier at a barbecue, when you are all a little bit pissed."

It was only a two-hour slot, so I had to work really fast. Nothing had been cleaned in a long time. There was a thin layer of grime on every surface and dust sticking to the grime. I kept scrubbing too hard and ruining the paintwork. On the bedside table, there was a photograph of them, the glass smashed. She was beautiful. The fact that he had kept the smashed photo was both heart-rending and a bit corny, a bit staged. I imagined him getting lucky – he was not a bad-looking dude – bringing a girl home and, out of respect for her, putting the photo face down.

He sat in the living-room, chain-smoking. His answer-phone kept going off. An annoyed woman, saying, "You have to deal with this. Grow up. Get a lawyer. Let's do this nicely." I had an iPod in my ears but it was switched off, so I could hear the messages while pretending to listen to music.

After the two hours were up, I walked into the living-room. He had smoked about fifteen cigarettes. I said, "You know in the bathroom, there is all this, um, woman stuff. Do you want it?"

"She might want it. Or do you want it?"

"No, thank you."

I wanted to say, it's a wife-leaving thing. You wouldn't understand. But as I saw him light up his sixteenth cigarette, I knew he understood all too well.

Chapter Eleven

American country singers. I go my whole life oblivious to them, then two come along in rapid succession. The second one was a troubadour, just about to break the UK. I was sent to interview her, and once again I thrust myself into fan-girl mode, forming a fast and easy bond. We were about the same age. We liked the same music, including hers, and we had some common reference points. We had both hung out in Washington Square Park with a guy who threw pies at politicians and other public figures who needed ridiculing. We high-fived over the pie thrower, one of the last living Yippies. She was quirky and irreverent, and had a plain-speaking charm and, like the other singer, was humble and seemingly baffled by her growing popularity.

She played a small club in Finsbury Park, and we hung out after the gig. When the interview ran, I thought that would be the end of it, and she would take her guitar and rucksack and head off to Europe or the States. But she rang me and asked me if I would like to be her tour manager for her American tour in the autumn. I told her I didn't know how to be a tour manager and she said, "Oh, it's nothing. We just get to hang out. You make sure we get to the airport and gigs and stuff on time and that

I have all my instruments and water on stage. It's really the easiest job ever."

With a sell like that, I could hardly say no. All I had to learn was how to write out an itinerary, how to book travel tickets in advance, arrange accommodation, figure out how little we could live on per day and how to get her instruments from one place to the next legally. When I saw how tight the schedule was, how many different states we had to travel to, how many flights and train trips were involved, I did feel out of my depth. She kept telling me it was no big deal, just planes and trains and venues, she would do the actual performing, I just had to get her there. I should have known that anyone overly enthusiastic about how easy a job is is probably overselling it, and that there is a very fine line between enthusiasm and sheer desperation. But her manager said once I got into the rhythm of it, it would happen quite naturally. The main thing was to show up to places on time. I was very good at this, as one of my neuroses was being late.

The night before we flew to the States, we stayed on her boat. Her bed was in the front of the boat, with a skylight over it. I spent my last night in England for a while looking at the stars in Tottenham Hale, sleeping side by side with the folk singer. It was the only peaceful night I had with her.

Very early in the morning, her manager came and took us to the airport, and we boarded a plane for an eleven-hour flight to California. It was the longest flight I had ever been on, and I was just about to get really nervous when the folk singer asked, "Where do we sleep?" and I said I guessed in the chairs, and she said, "No, I can't do that." So, after the seat belt sign went off, she lay down in the tiny space in front of our seats and tried to sleep. Immediately a flight attendant said that this would not do, she had to get up. The folk singer got up and I could see she was furious. But she wasn't furious with the airline; she was furious with me. Couldn't I sort this out? Couldn't I get her an upgrade?

It struck me that this job was not going to be as easy as it had been described to me. We fidgeted, ignored our meals, took garlic pills (she'd heard somewhere that this could ward off airborne illnesses) and at one point, I suddenly remembered I had half a gram of speed secreted in my bra. About an hour before landing, I went to the loo and snorted the lot. Apart from making me jumpy and bad-tempered, it was brilliant for avoiding the popping of eardrums on slow descent. It just seemed to clear all passages, except my head, which was hopping and fucked.

We landed, cleared customs, had a driver meet us and checked into what would be the first of a series of pretty nice Sheraton Hotels. Of course, the first night I was up all night, so I felt a bit ropey the next day but, strangely, not anxious. I really was impersonating a tour manager and the only thing that convinced me I was doing something right and that it would be OK was that the singer was a difficult person to work with. It was known, if not widely, at least in our small touring party, which included a protest singer, a Central American band and the sound engineer, that the folk singer was moody and, like myself, had a history of psychiatric complaints. The difference between us (apart from her obvious talent and marketability and winning way with an audience) was that she felt she had been wrongly diagnosed, that it was the SYSTEM, that everyone else was crazy, not her.

A young reporter from *People* magazine wanted to profile her, but she would not cooperate and he followed us around across three states (Georgia, Louisiana and Texas), trying to get the story and file his copy. I felt his pain. I knew what it was like from that end, but I was powerless to make her speak to him. When we were in Georgia, I knew that we had about two hours to get our stuff together, get to the airport and get to the next state for the next gig. The *People* guy rang me, more pissed off than frightened for his job, and demanded an interview. "What kind of *bullshit* is this?" he wanted to know. She wasn't all that famous, this was *People*, for chrissake, not some stupid fanzine, did she not understand the importance of publicity? I said I understood, she was a bit tricky, but I would try my best to get her out of the room and into the lobby for the interview before we had to get to the airport. I rang her room. No answer. I went over to her room and thumped on the door. I said, "You gotta let me in, we have a situation. The guy from *People*, he really wants to talk to you, he's been following us around for three states, it's *People*, it's huge, you gotta do it."

She opened the door and looked at me gravely. She said, "You know, there is some heavy stuff going on here."

I said yes, there was, but she could make it all better by talking to the guy from *People*, and I would pack for her – her two pairs of black leggings and t-shirts, her garlic pills, her instruments – she just needed to get her ass down to the lobby and be apologetic.

She said, "No, you don't understand, there is a conspiracy." She said she had photographic evidence. And then she led me to her bed, which was covered in Polaroids of the wallpaper of the Sheraton. There were about 30 of them, from different angles.

I said, "OK, so instead of talking to the guy from *People,* you've been taking pictures of the walls."

She said, "Look at the insignia. I mean, really, look at it. What do you think it is?"

I studied the photographs, all of groups or single shots of the Sheraton logo, which was on everything. I said, "I think it's an S, which is the first letter of Sheraton. It's quite a boxy S, but it is an S for Sheraton, nonetheless."

She stroked her chin and said, "Look at it again. You don't think it looks like a swastika?"

I shook my head. "I've only seen photographs of them, but no. It looks entirely different. Am I right in thinking that you believe this hotel chain is run by Nazis? I think it's a mistake. You've got to talk to *People*, then we have to get to the airport. Now!"

I threw her things in a bag and we ran downstairs to meet the now-furious guy from *People.* They sat at a table while she lied pointlessly about her age and real name, which were very easy to find out. My anxiety was starting to kick in, big time. I needed sedatives. I knew in the next state we were going to, New Mexico, we would be staying with a friend of a friend, not in a hotel. They would have a doctor, or at least a medicine cabinet I could explore.

Her first gig there was at a juvenile detention centre for girls. Her US publicist felt it was a good thing to do some charity gigs in young people's prisons. This upped my anxiety level even more, for I knew that in prisons, to get from one part to the next, you had to find a guard to open a whole bunch of locks.

After the gig, the singer and I were supposed to have lunch with the kids in the mess hall. We lined up with our trays. All the food was unidentifiable, mushy, reconstituted. I looked over at the singer, who was nodding in sympathy and telling her own tales of incarceration. I sat silently, drawing fork lines in my mashed potato. All the while I was thinking, no, I cannot identify with you lot. You are in big trouble. The girl passing me the salt may have taken out her own parents with a pitchfork and a hammer, but you know, it was THE SYSTEM. Not her fault. Rictus grin, smiles of empathy, bowels turning to water with every mouthful of mush, I felt nothing, except an urgent need to get out of the prison. I could not feel their pain. Only my own.

The singer's behaviour became more erratic, sort of poor woman's diva. She'd pass me a note in the van (for she had stopped talking to me): "Get me 200 pencils and little pieces of paper and make sure the pencils are sharpened." So I sharpened all these pencils and gave her them for the next gig and she looked at me as if I were insane. Another note: "What are these for?" I scribbled back, "YOU TELL ME!"

She fired me a few times. Then she hired me again. I kept going back, as it felt like a test of endurance. During one of the sackings, when we were in New York, I took a room in a hotel in the theatre district, a dive. Roaches everywhere. Peeling paint and wallpaper. But affordable. I literally did not know if I was going to get any more money, if I would be hired again.

I got ill. Roasting hot one moment, freezing cold the next, I stayed in the room for a few days quaking with chills and fever, then went to stay with my mother in Queens. Shellshocked and still ill from the tour, I felt out of place. My mum had taken a lodger, a friend of mine who had become a great friend to her, and my presence was upsetting the nice vibe of the set-up. I could see my mum was really happy, she had a best friend, and they did things together and had a routine going. I just didn't belong there. I wasn't even sure if I belonged in England any more. But I remember feeling that I had to get back there, and I'd decide whatever would happen next once I arrived.

* * *

Almost as soon as I got back to my lodgings in London, the girl I was sharing with said I had to leave and I probably knew why. I had heard these words before. There was something I was doing that made me hard to live with, something hugely unlikeable. I was never going to be one of those people others would describe as "quiet, kept herself to herself…" but I didn't set out to deliberately irritate people either. Clearly I was a pain in the arse. This seemed to come naturally. The on-the-surface reason for my necessary departure from the flat was that I didn't keep my room tidy. Her mother came over one day

with her best friend and they cleaned the place from top
to bottom, kind of as a hobby, all the while asking me if
I had ever dusted, if I had ever pushed the Hoover round.
They called each other Mrs Mop and kept saying, "Good
Heavens!" after, say, revealing a dustball behind the sofa.

It was not difficult for me to reconcile their jolly posh-
ness and vigour for "mucking in" with what they were
actually doing. For them it was a game, sporting. Being of
use! Ha ha. Little did any of us know that there would be
a time I did this very thing, every day.

Once again, the alacrity with which I was forced to
move appealed to me. I was really getting into throwing
all my things into the back of a cab and chain-smoking (I
rarely smoked, except in taxis, because you were allowed
to back then). And I would move from A to B, all my stuff
sliding around the back of the taxi. Holly GoDarkly, on
the move again.

Cleaning, London 2015
THE AMBULATORY SHAVERS

I HAVE A REGULAR GIG in Tech City, near Old Street. Eternal students, rich parents. I do not begrudge those who are rich and lacking plans or direction. At least, I didn't... until this particular job.

Two Saudi brothers, in a flat that could be measured in acres. They are in their mid-20s, one studying business, the other... seemingly lost in a sea of women, booze and drugs. The copy of the Koran his father sent lies on top of some angry red-print rent arrears letters. The flat is entirely white and these are the hairiest dudes I have ever seen: mono-browed, chest hair of rug-like density and rogue black wiry curls springing unbidden from ears, nose, back of neck. One is slightly shorter than the other. That is the only difference.

The floors and bathroom fittings are all white marble, all covered in hair that has been shaved off, in trails leading to the open-plan kitchen, the bedrooms, the living area. I am puzzled about why the hair is not in one place. They shave with portable electric razors, walking, talking on their mobiles. I dub them the ambulatory shavers and as I hoover up I wonder if I should leave some leaflets on waxing underneath the mountains of pizza and kebab shop fliers.

Everything about this gig sucks, starting with the receptionist who rings me in and says, "The cleaner is downstairs. Shall I send it up?" Maybe it is a mere grammatical slip, English clearly not being her first language. "What do you mean, it? Do I look like a pizza?" As she seems about to answer me, possibly in the affirmative, I wave her off and say, "Never mind. 'It' is fine. Works for me."

The flat smells funky, unaired, overheated. Sheets that have hosted various sexual acts are bunched up on the floor, which is also littered with dropped pound coins and even some notes. Every surface in the bedrooms and bathrooms has some sort of product for the removal of hair. Creams, lotions, tweezers, razors... these brothers shed hair and money; the hair must be vacuumed up, and the money placed in little piles so they know nothing has been nicked. You never know if dropped money is an honesty test or just... dropped money.

They never talk to me. They just grunt, point, play video nasty games and shave. They do this week in and week out and I am constantly emptying the Hoover of all the hair, gagging on the intimate body smells rising from the bed linen. I am about to jump ship – this after a particularly miserable clean when they have both been up partying all night, eating greasy food and drinking neat spirits. I decide I will go one last time, and then make my excuses and bolt.

But something changes two weeks later. They cancelled a week because they were away. And next time I show up the shorter shaver answers the door and it is apparent he is in a state. I ask if he has been away and he says, "Two of us went away, but only I came back." In broken English, he tells me that his brother, with his drinking and smoking and takeaway-pizza habit, has been held under parental house arrest in Saudi Arabia, having not cracked open a business study book, having not made any money, having not been a good Muslim, and having acquired a disease that required strong antibiotics and creams, which are still sitting on his bedside cabinet of shame. I feel oddly sorry for him, for both of them.

I notice… that he has not shaved. The stubble is at least a day old. This is serious. I should say something, show some sympathy. Get him a new razor or something. He is just a kid, lost in a sea of hair and money.

Towards the end of the clean, when he is loafing about the kitchen area, making coffee, I say, "You know, he might come back."

"What do you know?" he bellows, slapping down his coffee mug so hard that all the coffee spills out. He makes no attempt to wipe it up.

In "it" mode, I wipe up the coffee, and mumble to myself, "I know… nothing."

Chapter Twelve

The room I found was in the same road where I had lived before, in Hackney. It ticked all my "I'm not fussed" boxes: small, cheap, damp, smelly, covered in a thin sheen of grease and dust. To move into a dirty flat is a marvellous thing. All you can do is make it cleaner.

None of the furniture had been changed since the 50s. I put my books in the kitchen area cupboards, my suitcase on top of the wardrobe and decided to brighten the place up with lots of houseplants, which I named, for the illusion of not living entirely alone. Fiona the fern. Mikey the money tree. Spike the spider. Mad plant lady is somewhere on the spectrum of mad cat lady. I was working my way down.

I stocked up on 50-pence pieces for the gas metre, still vaguely suspicious of the explosion theory as put to me by my first London landlord, and got some essentials from the shops in Upper Clapton Road. Blankets. A kettle. A saucepan. Hot-water bottles. One for the midsection, one for the feet.

I cleaned the bedsit from top to bottom. There is nothing like that first clean, the big change from before to after. Sugar-soaped the walls to remove tobacco stains. Beat the rugs. Threw out loads of things. As I cleaned and scrubbed, I felt the cold leave me. Cleaning gave a feeling that if I started from the outside in, if I put things on the outside in order, then the messed-up things inside me would also take some sort of shape or order, by osmosis. This is probably a milder, off-spectrum, lazy girl's version of OCD. I feel compassion for those whose lives are ruled by cleaning rituals, but the practical part of me thinks, why not get paid for it?

So, yes, I loved that first big, novelty clean, but was easily bored and distracted by maintenance. (Later in life, I preferred the one-off agency cleans over the steady gigs. They made a bigger difference, and there was never time to develop the humdrum familiarity of routine.)

Once I had smartened the place up, I could see myself living there, alone, for ever. There are worse ways to get old. And getting old beats never growing up in the first place. At 29, living in a bedsit, with no steady income, no significant relationship and no map for life at all, never growing up seemed a distinct possibility.

During these bedsit years, I was working for a record company in West London. It was a small, friendly label with a lovely team of co-workers and, though I enjoyed the job itself, I found the long bus-and-three-Tube commute triggered my panic attacks again. I had met a new boyfriend as well, a very nice fella who was not quite over his last girlfriend; he still kept a photo of her in his room. She was striking, and I remember him telling me the photo had been taken on a boat to France, when she had been seasick. To look that good, seasick... I sort of knew where I was from the start, just no match for this woman who broke his heart. He was… uncomplicated. I was hardwired for complications and laboured explanations as to why I didn't like going out places, why I didn't feel OK a lot of the time. Really, what young guy wants to hear that shit?

I felt it was definitely going to be another case of "It's not you, it's me", a line I had trotted out before. I had the whole thing down to a fine, self-pitying art. I'd break up with the guy and somehow blame him for not trying harder, or at all, to win me back. But then this guy introduced me to another guy, who was to become my best friend, Paul. It was Paul who consoled me through this break-up, as he was also nursing a wounded heart. In fact, getting over breaking up with this guy, with Paul at my side, was way more fun than trying to have a relationship. It was so easy. We'd go round to each other's flat and play records and maybe get a little hammered, and play more records. Our record collections were almost identical, something that was very important to me at the time. Neither of us were interested in the other in a physical way, though it was plain to see he was incredibly good-looking.

Still, my bedsit land idyll was starting to crumble. I started using large chunks of my salary on minicabs to avoid the three Tube changes I needed to make to get to work. I went for acupuncture, which made me cry but didn't stop the horrors. I switched to liquid Stemetil – the English version of the Compazine I had taken in America – for my stomach, because it was absorbed faster, but got into the sorry habit of swigging it straight from the bottle, which made me shake again, the way I used to in Boston. In higher doses it is used to treat psychosis, and it can twist the tongue up and make it hard to pronounce words. I was stumbling over my words, though I do remember that, after one very powerful acupuncture session, I had a moment of false clarity, a fake-news version of cause and effect. I had convinced myself that the last boyfriend and his general indifference, bordering on relief, about our break-up, was the reason I needed to take so much medicine. In a post-acupuncture pique of melodrama, I went round to the ex's flat and starting lobbing all my empty medicine bottles at him, partially because my mouth was too fucked to get the words out properly, but also because I kind of liked throwing things. He, in turn, put two and two together and came up with five, and was worried that I had taken all the medicine at once. Paul came round to my place later and, after a couple of beers and records, he said, "Oh yeah, I was supposed to ask you something. Have you like, OD'd? _____is worried that you took all your medicine at once."

"No, but thanks for asking, on his behalf." In all my anxiety and general malaise with most of what life had offered so far, I had never felt inclined to top myself. I was too curious to see what might happen next. I kept taking days off work, so many that the bosses called me in for a talking-to and, though they were friendly and sympathetic, I could not explain why I had so many sick days, because I could not understand why I felt so sick. I was unable to get Valium in sufficient amounts to function as a normal person. My GP during this period was OK about giving me anti-sickness medicine, and my hopes rose when he finally gave me something for the anxiety too, but they were betablockers, useless to me, giving me low blood pressure and double vision. At one point I had to go over to Ireland to interview a singer and, necking twice the suggested amount of pills, I spent the whole trip seeing two of everything, trying to decipher which was the real thing or person, and which was a figment of my double vision. During another trip to Paris, this time as a journalist, to interview Lenny Kravitz, I had such an enormous panic attack at the airport, I hid in a janitor's cupboard until our flight was called – this after sending the press officer out to get me Valium, which she somehow managed to do. Like my friend Julie said, I was a well-travelled agoraphobic; but, with no steady supply of drugs, I had to stop doing press trips. It got to the point where I was lucky to get over to West London to work. That freakish, fickle, useless terror was once again taking over my life, informing its decreasing geography. The only fun bits of my life back then were all to do with Paul.

Well-read, funny, a wonderful storyteller, Paul could lift me out of any bad mood and magically seemed to be able to stem the bouts of anxiety and depression I had been sinking into with alarming frequency. On any night out with a group of friends, my eyes searched the room for Paul. If Paul were there, I could stay. It would be all right. That stuff in the Bible about perfect love casting out fear, I have never found to be the case, though I grew to love Paul deeply, without ever falling in love with him in the romantic sense: nobody made me laugh like he did, and nobody till then had made me feel safe like he did. As our friendship deepened, I came to know something approaching a state of relative calm. It's not as if he had planned it, or did anything special or that he was particularly Zen himself. I just knew that being around him felt better than not being around him. He was a human talisman. My lucky socks.

He talked a lot about his ex-wife, who lived in America. He had dreams of getting back with her, and there was nothing I wanted more than for my now best friend to be happy. So I told him to go get his girl, go to America, just show up, and get her back. It would mean not getting to see him as much, but the way I figured it, he'd bring her back to England and we could all be friends together.

The night before he left, we went to our local dive, which he called the Killer, because people were always getting killed in there. We drank, we danced, we did karaoke and had some kind of heart-to-heart, with me promising that if he did this grand-surprise gesture, flying the ocean and winding up on her doorstep, she (the ex-wife) would take him back. Me, I had nothing much to look forward to. It was building up to Christmas and New Year. I would be on my own, no festive plans, but it felt OK. Paul would be back, hopefully with his wife again, in the New Year.

During this in-between time, with people flying out of London, luggage overstuffed with presents, the city goes quiet. It was during this period that Paul's other best friend asked me out on a date. I'd seen this guy about but, for one reason or another, we rarely saw Paul at the same time. I liked this guy a lot. He was funny, out-of-my-league handsome and had such an impenetrable Belfast accent I could only make out every third word he said. We went out to the pub, to a gig, somewhere else, I can't remember. It was just a whirlwind of laughter and fun and profound happiness. Here was my surrogate Paul, only better, because I was falling in love with him. He was the first person I thought of in the morning, the last person I thought of before I went to sleep.

All these years later, for this was the start of 1991, I still love that little window of time between Christmas and New Year, the end of one party and the beginning of another, when nothing much happens. London is stuffed, replete, hushed, hungover, waiting for the next round of excess. People sit heavily on sofas, binge-watching telly, reading about New Year diets in magazines while chomping on chocolates. Those of us with no ties are free to roam the drizzly, snow-melty streets, and fall in love, as I did.

Cleaning, London 2015
THE DEAD ZONE

THIS FLAT BELONGS TO A Russian financial whiz-lady and her husband who travels a lot for work. Christmas is over. There is a Lush gift basket of heavily scented toiletries, unopened, under a pile of pine needles from a falsely advertised "no needle drop" tree. A food hamper from Selfridges. A top-of-the-range scented candle. A Nigella cookbook. Presents you give to people you don't really know, just in case they got you one. They are having a clean for a guest and a small New Year's Eve party.

Every bit of the small flat is crammed with stuff from her mother country and all the countries they have visited. She sits on the sofa, talking tight-lipped into her mobile phone, so as not to jiggle the clear face mask she is wearing, to unblock pores. At one point during the clean, she peels it off in one big face-shaped strip, as if she is pulling her face off. She does this while watching telly and filing her nails. She leaves the face peeling on the table. I say, "Um, would you like me to discard your, um, face thing?" And she laughs and says, no, she will do it herself, later. She puts it in the nut bowl, the crumpled gel nestling among the Brazil nuts. Apart from this one very wrong thing in the wrong place, everything is tidy, every surface has its own special internet-purchased cleaning fluid – for marble, for brass, for stainless steel, for ceramic hobs.

In the bedroom, the woman's bedside table is full of Russian Orthodox icons and I am afraid if I move them to dust them, some sort of religious karma will be disrupted. His side of the bed has got a full box of my favourite American tranquilliser. Bloody Xanax, again. Deliver me once more from temptation. God, or drugs? This has been a problem of recent adult life: spirits, or spiritual, God, or vod? I lift everything up, dust and put it back down. Will he miss one Xanax? Yes, probably. I would. So I leave them alone, but keep staring at them, my forbidden drug porn. Then I dust the icons, mini three-fold, gilt-framed pictures of Russian saints, and try to put them back in the same place. I look at the Xanax again and count them – 20. An even number, and in blister strips. He'd notice if one went missing. How would it feel, to take a Xanax on New Year's Eve, and then drift off to a Narcotics Anonymous meeting? Probably pretty good. So I leave the box, the pretty lilac oblong strips and go back to her side of the bed, kneel down, and start to pray. I don't know the names of any Russian Orthodox saints, so I just call them all Olga. "St Olga, please save me from the temptation on the other side of the bed. Please save me, and you'll understand this, being Russian, from buying a last-minute bottle of Russian Standard vodka at Sainsbury's before I go home." I am praying audibly, and I really don't care if she walks in at this point, because better to be caught praying than nicking drugs.

When my job is almost done, I ask her if there is anything else and she says, no thank you; she wishes me a Happy New Year and asks what I am doing. I don't tell her

my plan, which is to go to a Narcotics Anonymous meeting and tell a room of strangers that, confronted with a
box of my favourite drugs, I didn't take any. And as I walk
to the meeting that night, I am glad I am not going to a
party where I will not be able to get drunk or have fun.
These days, I am grateful for the smallest things. Watching a
woman take her face off, without being off my face.

Chapter Thirteen

In our early courtship, my boyfriend and I moved from my bedsit, where we curled up on a single bed most nights, to what was then called "rooms". These were rooms we rented in a flat with a communal toilet and hallway, shared with an elderly man called Roy. The best thing about this flat was that it came with a kitsch home bar, one of those semi-circular 60s things that now go for a small fortune in vintage shops. Interior design magazines would call it a statement piece. I just thought it would be dead handy for the bar to be in your own home. Less staggering distance to the bedroom or bathroom. But I was not drinking that heavily – yet. I had ways and means of getting what I needed pharmaceutically, without having to top up with alcohol to potentiate the effects of pills.

Potentiate, to make stronger, was one of the words I learned from the leaflets that come with prescription drugs. If the leaflet said, "Avoid alcohol which will potentiate the effect of _____(tranquilliser), I would, in years to come, immediately go out and get some booze. It was like the pharmaceutical equivalent of a shampoo and conditioner in one. Why just get tranquil if you can get tranquil and a bit pissed, and then forget about both, and everything that happened in between. I was not doing this at this point, but eventually, the potential to potentiate became too tempting to resist. They call addiction a cunning and baffling "disease" because you wind up doing stuff that would make no sense to normal people. I was not that crazy, yet. I just had crazy potential.

The bar was like a grown-up version of a doll's house or a Wendy house. I loved standing behind it, dispensing real drinks to imaginary customers. The Wendy Bar, mark one – for there was a second bar a few flat moves later, was the start of an elaborate joke that went horribly wrong.

If I got home from work before my boyfriend, I would make sure I had some sort of cornball muzak cued up on the stereo, say, Andy Williams' "Music to Watch Girls By". I would pour us both drinks and we would sit there, like somebody's parents in the 60s, getting slightly loaded while discussing who was coming for dinner. At that time. it was in the realm of funny ha ha, as opposed to the funny peculiar it was to become, and later just peculiar and then just... me being a pisshead.

We liked entertaining, and in our core group of close-knit friends, Paul was the closest, being our mutual best friend. The big "go get yer girl" gesture I had encouraged him to make had not worked out. So the happy trio I had envisaged – Paul, his wife and me – became Paul, his guy best friend and his girl best friend. The set-up was convenient but also potentially explosive. There was a built-in reason to never fall out with either of them: it would fracture more than one relationship. It was very important to me, I think to all of us, that we all stayed on the same side. Years later, when Paul died and I went crazy, I went back to that line my mother had, about a bit of her dying when my father did. The difference was, Paul was never my husband or even my lover. I just loved him... way too much.

And here is an inconvenient truth about loving someone way too much. If and when they die before you, you can find yourself loving the memory as much as, if not more than, the real person in real life, for you edit out anything human or fallible about them. The hunger for their company, in death, surpasses the hunger for their company in real life. The fact that we were never "in love" or lovers made me think my love for Paul was a very pure form of love, but in reality it was only pure in its supposed exclusivity (and it was not exclusive, for Paul was loved hard, by many) and ultimate selfishness. Never choose your dead beloved over your living beloved. Because, you know, they won't be aware of it, while those who are still living will be very aware, painfully aware, that your heart lies with the dead.

When I fell happily but nervously pregnant with my first child, my obsession with Paul waned only slightly, as I got busy preparing to be a mum to this little life inside me. My boyfriend, later my husband, and I went into parenthood besotted with the notion, besotted with each other. Pregnancy, although sicky and uncomfortable in the initial weeks, energised me in ways that had previously felt elusive. I was constantly hungry, happy, horny and hopeful. It was a wonderful nine-month holiday from real life. I loved the fact that there was a little person inside me, that I was taking up more physical space than I ever had. During an appointment at the surgery when I was 20 weeks gone, drug-free and feeling fabulous, my GP called his partners in to examine my hard, swollen belly. He said, "This is exactly what a 20-week pregnancy should look like. She is perfectly 20 weeks pregnant." Having never been perfectly anything, particularly healthwise, in my life, I felt that being halfway through a pregnancy was my perfect place to be. I felt that if my problems with anxiety and pills were in part some sort of genetic imprint, perhaps I could breed it out, with a man who was as calm and happy as my boyfriend, her father.

The first year after I had my daughter was bliss. I had never known a love so compelling, so instant, so feral, so possessive. This was it, the human form of the perfect love that cast out fear. She was a very happy and portable baby. I went to show her off in the States when she was four months old. I just popped her in a little sling on my front and off we went.

When she was about a year old, we moved to new flat. Our present one was too small and our means too mean to get anything much bigger, but we did find an ex-council place and soon after the move I fell pregnant again. The second pregnancy was less easy than the first. The rhythm my daughter and I had developed, just being together all the time, was disrupted by fatigue, nausea and a sudden realisation that the days were very long.

But when my son was born, quickly, with little fuss, in 1996, I experienced the same surge of love and protectiveness that I had done following the birth of my daughter. The sheer busyness and exhaustion of looking after two small children seemed to displace any feelings of anxiety, any cravings for drugs. We had a wide social circle and a huge extended family. There were parties and children's activities and play dates and playgroups. There were moments of profound happiness doing the most mundane things, like sitting on the edge of the sandpit in the park, watching my kids get totally lost in a game of pirates; or buying the inevitable second ice cream on the South Bank, the first having been dropped almost instantly by very small, impatient hands; or sniffing the tops of their damp, clean heads after a long bath. And there were times of sheer tedium, turning gently blue in the pissed-in pool at Britannia Leisure Centre, or losing the feeling in my fingertips after an obligatory extra half-hour in the playground in Clissold Park, in December, to wear them out. These two little people were so easily pleased. My life, thank fuck, I thought, was no longer my own. There was just no TIME to do drugs.

Soon, however, this period of domestic bliss was shattered. We lived on an estate called the Mount, though someone had rubbed off the M and O and scrawled a C over it. Our upstairs neighbour had severe mental health issues, but not severe enough to be considered a risk to herself, her three sons, or her neighbours. She was technically "care in the community" though the community did not care for her. She had the vacant gaze, wild hair and stupefied stagger of someone on heavy medication – a look I was to cultivate myself in later years. She disposed of her youngest son's nappies by chucking them off the balcony, and when I complained about it, and about the fact that her sons had returned a football they'd borrowed from my kids, punctured, I found out the hard way that you never, ever complain about anything to anyone crazier than yourself. I got payback in the form of intimidation and threats on a daily basis after that. Why hadn't I just shut the fuck up about the football? Was it worth all this grief? Despite my theory of real-life problems displacing my default free-floating anxiety, the tension between this woman and me sent fresh, hellish ripples of panic and fear through my, till then, fairly happy domestic world of kiddies, boyfriend and friends.

In addition to the psycho upstairs, there was a heavy atmosphere about the estate, which ran along what was then known as Murder Mile. Lots of guys standing close together and exchanging drugs for money with handshakes. Lots of guys coming over to our bit of the estate, cut off from the main road, to take a piss. My boyfriend, having grown up in 70s Belfast, took the sensible approach of no eye contact, head down, don't draw attention to yourself, don't cause a fuss.

But I was wild, incandescent with rage. Why did my kids have to grow up like this? Who were these people, these fuckers, throwing dirty nappies on our teeny bit of London? Pissing on our bike sheds? Selling drugs (not my kind of drugs, respectable prescription drugs, but hard stuff, proper narcotics)? I would get into fights with her upstairs, and then beat a retreat to our maisonette, my ill-defined terror suddenly taking real, human shape.

Normally, I would have been straight on the tablets, but under the illusion that motherhood would cure everything that was ever wrong with me, I had let my supply run out. I told the pissing men to put it back in their trousers and fuck off. Just going to and from the shops became a trip fraught with danger, some real, some imagined. Her upstairs would be smoking on her landing, waiting to hurl insults and/or garbage at me when I returned.

A new surgery opened where the petrol station used to be. I liked the poetry of it. One kind of fuel for another. It was great for the sort of fuel I needed to keep it together. Increasingly, the notion of a "just in case" stash was broadening to include not only the psycho-geographical landscape of my mind – the false fears that live in the primitive brain – but also the real dangers of our neighbourhood. "Just in case something happens on the estate." Something was always happening on the estate. I would have latched onto any excuse. That first consultation with GP at the new surgery involved very little persuasion on my part. "I have two children under five, and we live on Murder Mile and I have a long history of anxiety and depression." The GP barely looked up from his computer. "What do you need? Fives? Tens?" BINGO!

With a steady supply of drugs coming in, all I needed was a ready excuse to take them. In my unquiet mind, going out to dinner was as nerve-racking a prospect as getting physically threatened by a neighbour. Just as anxiety is the great leveller of all emotions, thoughts and actions, reducing every stimulus, in my case, to a neurological haze of needless nausea and pointless paralysis, so its supposed palliative eventually reduces every response to a blunted blur of over-sedated inaction. Who would want to feel... nothing? People whose default state of being is a sort of stage fright of the soul... where every moment of their lives, apart from being unconscious or nearly so, is terrifying. There is no such thing as comfortably numb, in the world of the neurotic. There is tolerable, but never comfortable. Normal people, whom I have met, have trouble understanding this. "Valium?" they say. "Oh, I think I may have taken one for a long-haul flight..." One? May have???

The rest of our time living in that flat, I was in a nearly permanent state of stolid sedation, a Valium fog, disrupted only by rows with her upstairs, the frequent wail of sirens, and on one occasion by a shooting right in front of our building. My kids were watching a video of the musical *Cats*. I heard the shots and went to the window and saw a guy slumped over his steering wheel. A girl staggered out of the car, her leg soaked in blood. My daughter was belting along with the video, pretending to be a dancing, singing cat and going, "Memmmmooriess...", and I thought, wildly, "God, you are *so adorable*... but there seems to be a situation outside..." I think I knew I was going to see something hideous, traumatising, and I wanted to plant the image of my kid, singing along to *Cats* in my head: let me remember this, rather than what I am about to see.

I went to get a towel to wrap around the girl's leg. I climbed out of our window – it was the quickest way to get to her, and walked over to the car. By this time there was a crowd, but nobody seemed to know what to do. I peeked into the window and saw the driver had been shot in the head and was dead. The stuff inside his head was now all over the dashboard. "Focus," I thought. "Don't take a mental snapshot of this. Just think of your cute kid, singing Andrew Lloyd Webber, and all this will be cleared away in a short time." This mental trick did not work. Whenever I hear the soundtrack to *Cats* I think of blood and gore and dead people.

A helicopter landed in the road to airlift the woman to hospital. There were cops and medics everywhere. My kids thought it was like a big party and my daughter got the biscuit tin and went out onto the lawn, offering Jammy Dodgers to cops, hoodies, rubberneckers and the ambulance guys. The day after, a cop came over to ask me loads of questions I could not answer. Did I see the gunmen? Did I hear the shots? How many? What happened to the towel? I had no idea. I was lost in *Cats* and drugs. Her upstairs just surveyed the scene from her balcony. After the cops left our flat, she called me a white vampire for cooperating with them. The guy who died, the guys who shot him, were her "brothers". Not her real brothers, just street brothers. My boyfriend and I agreed this was the final warning, that it was time to go, and to go quickly. I remember staring out of the window that night, under the streetlights, which made everything look filmic and pretty: there was some gigantic cleaning machine, pouring industrial-strength bleach over the whole crime scene, erasing it all. The guy operating the machine was whistling... all in a day's work.

Cleaning, London 2015
BOG STANDARD

I USE BLEACH, ALWAYS, IN TOILETS. People tell me to use Ecover, and I do, but only after the bleach. I bring it to every cleaning job. Nothing works as well as bleach. Bleach makes everything smell like an over-chlorinated swimming pool. It stings my eyes, irritates my nose, and makes me feel like I am sacrificing my health, and the environment as a whole. I picture the guy from the council mopping up blood from crime scenes with gallons of bleach. How much bleach does he inhale on a daily basis? Will he die a slow and painful death in an iron lung, wishing he could be taken out quickly by the gunshot-style death he is employed to clean up after?

The agency sends me to two jobs, two hours each. I take my bleach to them both. Job one is local, a home loft space. A woman answers the door and asks if I am with the crew. I say I am the cleaner and she says, "I didn't ask for a cleaner", and I say, "Well, maybe the crew did," still not having a clue who the crew are. It turns out they are using the woman's vast NYC-style open-plan loft kitchen space for an advert for a healthy juice. She tells me to sit down, she has to get her kids up for school, and I sit on the vast grey Conran sofa as she goes up a gappy staircase. She is holding a tray with two bowls of muesli and two glasses of orange juice. A mum who gives her kids breakfast in bed.

Christ, rub it in, why don't ya, you and your functional family and steady income. She says, taking the steps at two at a time, "I rent my place out for adverts and film shoots. Pays the mortgage."

Within minutes, about fifteen people come into the space. They have all the stuff – props, signs, food, cameras, mics, lights – and they all get to work, everyone knowing exactly what they are doing and doing it fast and well. They take out all her lovely, slightly dusty things – tins of strange Moroccan spices, items I've seen on Nigella Lawson's cookery shows – and put their heavily branded stuff in. All touches of reality need be removed to give the advertised product the money shot.

I sit on the sofa. The woman has forgotten me, what I am there for, or what I am not there for. I find the woman who has actually hired me, the woman who is producing the advert. I ask, "What would you like me to do?" and she replies, "I'm not really sure. Clean something, I guess." Then the mum comes down and I ask her, "Is anything messy, or does anything actually need a clean?"

She thinks. Really, everything is immaculate. Maybe I can pour some bleach down the small lav at the bottom of the stairs and make sure the towel is clean. I go down the stairs and find the loo: immaculate, as is the towel. I pour bleach down the lav and scrub some Vim into the small shiny hand basin.

I go back up the stairs as slowly as possible. I've been booked for two hours. Only 40 minutes have passed. Everyone is in their 20s, and they are all speaking this filmy language. I tell the director I have cleaned the loo. She says,

"Great, you can go now. Don't worry, we'll pay you for the two hours." Later that day I see she has given me a five-star review, for cleaning an already clean toilet.

The second job, a few hours later, is in a railway arch in the Eastest of East London. Once there I am introduced to a boy just a few years older than my son. He has set up a food delivery company. I recognise the logo. Boys on bikes, weaving along the pavements with huge boxes perched on the back. . . I am not to go near the kitchen. My job is to vacuum the offices and clean the office toilet.

The vacuuming noise immediately annoys all the office workers, who are giving me cut-throat signs as I clean around large stacks of papers and boxes. Down in the loo, it is almost gratifyingly filthy. I do the toilet, the tiles and the floor, and set off a nuclear air freshener explosion by spraying the entire contents of a vanilla-scented air freshener can in the tiny room. Again, the whole job is over in well under an hour. Everyone is so damned young, so damned busy. Making food and sending it out to other people so damned young and too damned busy and tired to cook. Me, I am the old drug addict cleaning the toilet, watching the world race by.

Chapter Fourteen

When we moved into our second ex-council flat in Stoke Newington, I noticed what at first felt like a wonderful and communal spirit. There was a run-down playground in the centre of the flats and all the children, all ages and sizes, would play together unsupervised. There were big kids looking after smaller kids, doing the sort of stuff parents would blanch at, like twisting the swing so tightly round and then letting it fly into a whirling dervish, with the kid on the swing getting so dizzy and disorientated he or she would dismount and fall down or puke. Boys, agile as monkeys, scaling the scaffolding for works about to be done, or never done, or just plain abandoned. Seven-year-old girls pushing babies (not dolls, real babies) around in prams. This was a rice-cake-carrot-stick-and-hummus-free zone. It was shared-out multi-packs of Golden Wonder, eaten so quickly as to be inhaled, then chucked down anywhere but in a bin. There were no rules about screen time, about quality time, about orchestrated play dates. Young girls, skimpily clad, made a stage of the playground wall and did note- and dance-step-perfect renditions of songs like "No Scrubs" or anything by Destiny's Child, complete with salacious gyrations and gestures. There were kids with the blue-stained mouths of cheap ice lollies and the blood-red lips of a sweet called Toxic Waste. I thought I had died and woken up in child-rearing heaven. The kids were bringing themselves up, an idea that struck me as both old-fashioned – a kind of "Run along and play now, Mum has washing to do" approach – and also insanely irresponsible.

Where were the parents? Not on the balconies, keeping even half an eye on them. Was this neglect, or was this as nature intended? I decided to let my kids join in, with the proviso that our front door would always be open, and I would stick my head out every fifteen or 20 minutes to see that all was OK. A few doors down was a woman I called the young woman who lived in a shoe. So many different kids would file out of that flat, of all ages. I knew at least one of her kids was in jail and she had custody of his pit bull, who walked himself, usually depositing his doggy doings on our front doorstep.

At first, the other kids accepted my kids, who, racially, were in the minority, the estate being mainly populated by black and Turkish kids, and I thought, hurrah, multicultural Britain, I am living it, my kids are assimilating, all things being equal in the playground. Soon they all started to file into our flat – me with my open-door policy – and they'd congregate in my kids' room, inspecting their toys, negotiating swaps, doing dances on the beds. I'd pop in now and then offering them crisps or cheap ice lollies.

My boyfriend felt uneasy about the whole set-up. He asked, reasonably, why all the kids played at our flat and never anyone else's. I had no answer. I was glad they were under my roof, making a glorious mess. At least I could see what they were up to. Then, one of the kids called my daughter a "white bitch", and other insults, all prefaced by the word "white", came filtering through. This was uncharted territory for me. My black friends said these were one-off acts of prejudice, not institutional racism, which was what black kids and mixed-race kids experienced daily. I would have been well advised to shut the fuck up about it. But this non-problem triggered an anxiety response in my daughter.

She didn't want to play outside any more. Once sent to the corner shop for a loaf of bread, she came back half an hour later, accompanied by the shopkeeper, who had seen that she was in such a state of distress he had brought her home himself. I asked her what was wrong, and she said the kids didn't like her any more. They called her names. My son, meanwhile, was showing signs of developmental delay. He was too quiet. When I asked him what he did all day in nursery, he said, "I do puzzles." When I asked him who he did the puzzles with, he said, "I do puzzles. Me."

When I enquired about speech therapy at his school, I was made to feel that I was being hysterical, that he was just a quiet kid; in fact, I should count my blessings. Later, when it turned out he was hard of hearing, a condition that could be fixed easily with a simple operation, I was relieved – his hearing could be restored. But I was still worried about my daughter. I worried that she had inherited my predisposition for anxiety. At least, that was the most forgiving explanation. The equally plausible and more disturbing version was that by nurture, I was turning her into an anxious child, that I was teaching her to be scared of stuff she didn't need to be scared of... that one day she would be scrabbling around for a doctor with an easy prescribing manner, just like mum.

The two of them played inside, with each other, or I would take them to the playground, to the soft-play centre, to the park, to the ice-skating rink, or the boating lake in Finsbury Park. I could no longer do the passive parenting thing. I could no longer just send them out to play. I had to be present and fully functioning in their lives, and my track record for being present and fully functioning in my own life was littered with prescriptions, pills and sick notes. No one had told me you could not call in sick, as a mum. It was 24-7, and the days seemed to start so very early, and end so very late.

Older parents were always telling me to "enjoy" this bit. It passed so quickly. Did it? For me, sometimes, it felt like time stood still. Half-term in particular. Half-term sometimes felt like life-term. It was never OK to say this aloud. Jokey banter, yes, but you could never say frankly that it could be hellish. The fact that I was playing chemical Russian roulette while looking after two children never occurred to me; or, if it did, I filed it under "I'll stop this when they leave home."

Around this time, I got a new GP who was a lot less handy with the prescription pad. The rules had changed. Valium could rarely be prescribed, and then only for a maximum period of one or two weeks. There was an international clampdown on overprescribing, overseen in this country by NICE, The National Institute for Clinical Excellence. I hated NICE. The word made me cringe, even when referring to the coconutty biscuit, the city in France, or the personality trait. NICE were the people who had made it really hard for me to get a steady supply of drugs – who had fucked up my safety net, when I most needed it, when my kids were in trouble. I took to the internet, buying strange pills from India, Bulgaria, Japan, Canada. Many, if not most, were fakes, but I found that if I topped up whatever fake or semi-real pill I was taking with a slug of vodka, it would pretty much numb the worst of my ever-increasing anxiety. I told myself I had proper fears, this time round. My kids were not OK.

It was a new sensation, to feel frightened for others. My fears had always been in the realm of the irrational, and up until now I had had little sense of real, personal danger. Now the outside world was posing threats that felt as big as, and certainly more real than, whatever my neurotic head could conjure up. Anxiety loves a cosmic petri dish, something that will multiply and magnify fearful thoughts with anything remotely, tangibly, justifiably a real source of concern. These feelings need to be quashed, not expressed. The pills I took were great for that, levelling everything out to a place somewhere between benign inactivity and slowness of physical movement and speech, to sheer stupefaction. We were not quite fucked, as a family, yet, but I was well on my way to messing my own life and health up and bringing the family down with me.

Our biggest asset, and it was a life-saving one, was our large group of friends in and around Stoke Newington. We had good friends around the corner, devout Muslims who both worked very hard and had early starts, so we got into the not-terribly-convenient-for-us-but-very-helpful-for-them arrangement of them dropping their two kids at ours, on the way to work, and me taking all four to school. It was one of those situations, and I have been in many, where there is no in-between. You are a good egg if you do the favour – oh, so reasonable at the time of being asked, sure, that's fine – but if you anticipate the potential problems, you are selfish. Particularly in light of their religious devotion and the fact that they were simply GOOD PEOPLE with GREAT KIDS, I could not say no. Not really.

Their devoutness fascinated me. Everything was pre-ordained. They just had to do all this stuff and NOT do all this other stuff and Allah would provide – well, Allah and London Underground, where Zach, the affable father of the family, drove the Victoria Line. We used to tease him because his whole family could ride the Tube for free, but he would drive them everywhere, even places that were short walks away. I asked him why he didn't let the family use the Tube.

"Are you mad? Do you know how dangerous it is?"

"But not your line? Victoria's got to be OK, if you're driving it..."

"It's not the driving. It's the track maintenance. Shocking."

"Well, how do you know nothing will happen to you?"

"I pray."

"What, while you are actually driving? You do the

whole bending-down thing?"

Here, he deftly changed the subject to Blackburn Rovers, his great passion. Looking after his well-behaved children in the morning proved a challenge from the start. I was usually just waking up from some drug-induced stupor. It took several cups of coffee just to blink. The two children would arrive just as we were getting out of bed, trying to find uniforms, lunches, make breakfast, etc. My increasing dependency on the internet was not helpful for drugs. I began to experience what I later found out was called a paradoxical effect. The drugs (sometimes they were the real deal; the vodka was always the real deal) would make me not calm, as intended, but very arsey and bad-tempered. I could tell that the kids, my friends' kids, if not my own, were getting to be a bit afraid of my wild mood swings. Eventually, we agreed the plan was not working out, as it complicated my already complicated mornings. And not long after we stopped this plan, I got a frantic phone call from a mutual friend. Zach, the jolly Tube driver and Rovers supporter, only in his early 30s, had dropped dead, not on the Tube, but playing football. Oh God, two fatherless children. A mother zapped into the twilight world of inconsolable grief. I knew that story... Here I could help. I wanted to help. In fact, I needed to help them more than they actually needed the services of a hysterical drug addict.

When I went to visit, I heard chanting and howling upstairs. My friend sat on the floor, eyes red-rimmed, praying, surrounded by female friends or family, all devout Muslims. She was following the Islamic mourning ritual of Idda, where the female mourner stays home for 40 days. This, I was told, was to ensure that if she happened to be pregnant (she was not) it would be sure to be the child of Zach.

I could see there was little I could do, and I did not understand all the customs of this form of grieving. I hugged her, bowed out and decided that I could not fix or save this family, that they had a huge support network and a devotion to a religion which seemed to really ease the pain of grief.

Like many people who have experienced death at close range, I was both entranced and repelled by a situation that brought back my own fatherless childhood. Then again, I didn't have the foggiest idea of how to deal with death outside the false comfort of a diazepam daze. My friend had Allah and family. I had drink and drugs. By this point I had so many secret stashes – at the back of the knickers drawer, in the side zipped pockets of a suitcase on top of the wardrobe, in countless purses, in a slim envelope tucked inside a copy of a magazine insert I had written myself – *101 Ways to Beat Stress* – and at the bottom of a box of folk music cassettes I never played any more. Later, I found that bottles meant for travel-sized amounts of shampoo or moisturiser held about a triple shot of vodka. My boyfriend kept telling me I smelled of alcohol. I told him it was that alcohol-based cleansing stuff for hands, which I applied lavishly to throw him off the scent of my breath. The thing about hiding is that, after a while, you just can't be bothered.

Cleaning, London 2011
THE WOMAN WITH ME

A TYPED INDEX CARD IN the window of the newsagent, where I used to buy my kids lurid sweets which turned their tongues and lips a virulent blue, says that a woman living about a two-minute walk from my bedsit is in need of general assistance. She has ME, and needs someone to come in for a few hours, twice a week, to clean, do some admin and help her with getting to appointments and to do other things that her ME makes it difficult for her to do herself.

The woman on the phone is all brisk efficiency, keen for me to come over as soon as possible once I tell her how close I live to her. I am drunk and have to sober up very quickly. I eat a tube of mints and drink one mug of instant coffee, and then just swallow some coffee granules with cold tap water, figuring it might work faster.

When I get to her house, she comes to the door in her wheelchair. She gives me the once-over, and I can see she is sizing my size up. My size is an English size 4, an American size zero, maybe not a good look for a job that requires a degree of robustness and sturdiness. We chat about ME, how debilitating it is, and how it is not recognised as a proper illness. Then she peers at me, and says, "It is very hard to find someone reliable. I have had several alcoholics apply for this job. It is not so much the smell of alcohol that gives them away, as the smell of mints." Before I can tell her that I am not one of those, that I just really like mints, she gives me a test task.

"Can you fold some sheets for me?"

Aw fuck, please don't let them be fitted sheets. I have seen a technique on YouTube but have forgotten it… something about fitting the corners into each other, in a diagonal manoeuvre.

It is, of course, a fitted sheet, and within seconds I am tangled up in the thing, like a cat trying to do origami. I am struggling under the sheet. OK, I can rescue this situation. Who are those dead people who wear sheets? Oh yeah, ghosts. Things that strike you as funny, when drunk, are hardly ever funny to other people. But I never learn this, while drinking. Under the sheet, I raise my arms and go, "Booo!"

She does not laugh. I manage to get the sheet folded into a semblance of a messy square, and put it on an empty chair.

"There is a technique", she says.

"Yes, I think I need a bit of a refresher course in that…" but my words ring hollow as she peers at me over her glasses, and I know then that not only have I not got the job, but I will be one of her legions of drunken minty applicants, and my heart goes out to her. She never signed up for ME, and there are some who might say, I never signed up for being an addict, but there was definitely a moment, lots of moments, when I had a choice. There is sometimes a moment of clarity, when you reach for the bottle at the top of the wardrobe, to fend off the morning jitters. When the jitters get so bad that you need to put a straw in the bottle and hold it steady, between your knees or on the floor, you have a second, sometimes longer than a second, when you think, "Why am I doing this shit?" But carry on doing it anyway.

Chapter Fifteen

Valium had been my sometimes faithful, often fickle friend since puberty, but an increasingly demanding, needy friend. It was taking up more space in my life – the getting of it, the sneaky taking of it, the supplanting of it, the obsession with it, the loud, angry, shaky, stomach-lurching withdrawal of the body when I could not get it when I needed it, which was, increasingly, most of the time. When I didn't have it, I was thinking about getting it. When I did have it, I was thinking about getting more. I could not seem to get it in amounts sufficient to bring me to my calm place. I was trying to figure out a way to be sedated enough to appear normal; but the sedative effect was becoming more elusive while the cognitive impairment was becoming more pronounced. In conversation, I started to repeat myself, with no notion that the story I was trying to tell was the story I had just told, and that it was hardly worth listening to the first time, let alone a second. It is a terrible thing to be a bore, and worse still, to bore yourself. My brain and mouth were unconsciously uncoupling. My good friend Helen, who would sit at my kitchen table, watching me chop vegetables for my kids' dinner while I was on the vodka tonics, and eventually, just the vodkas, would say quietly to me, "You've just told me that…" as I was repeating some not-worth-repeating anecdote. And this foxed me. "Um, what was it that I said?" There was a disconnect not only between the first and second versions, but a total memory failure with regards to what the story was in the first place.

Most addiction stories have an element of amateur chemistry. You experiment until you get the desired effect, or until you are so trashed, you forget what the desired effect ever was. As a child, one of my favourite birthday presents was a chemistry set. I loved the absolutely point-less experiments in the booklet that came with the box of chemicals and tubes "suitable for children aged ten plus". Float mothballs in a solution of vinegar! Grow your own penicillin on some Wonder Bread you leave in the coat closet for three weeks. Find the PH balance of your own spit. Now, as an adult, I *was* the pointless experiment. Take internally: become invertebrate, inarticulate, inebri-ated, incapable.

My late friend Drew had taught me the basics of self-medication after he was diagnosed with AIDS in the late 80s. Back then, it was a death sentence and, through various clinics and hospitals, he could get his hands on everything pharmaceutical. He told me that, if I could only get five milligrams, I should chase it with a long shot of vodka and it would act like ten milligrams. The more you drank, the stronger the effect of the pills. The fact that he could take industrial quantities of drugs and tell coherent, joined-up stories that were funny, enlightening and always entertaining, all the while he was taking the scenic route to death, made me think that I could possibly do the same.

While my in-body chemistry experiments were rendering me a bit slow on the uptake at best and plain boring, almost comatose, at worst, there was a nasty twist to my agoraphobic tendencies. The one safe place for an agoraphobic is home, but our home was beginning to feel unsafe. Crack dealers started operating out of the car park adjacent to our garden. They would sell crack and mend cars, throwing the spare car bits over our fence. With dogs shitting on our doorstep, and bits of battered metal and, at one point, a car battery, flying over the fence, I was beginning to feel under siege. The car battery flying over, while I was in the garden, led to an error of judgement I was immediately to regret. Incensed, I tried to throw it back, but I'd miscalculated the weight of the thing, and it teetered on the edge of the fence and fell back, opening up a big cut on my forehead. With blood gushing from my face, and hearing laughter on the other side, and my kids looking all kinds of terrified, I was just pressing a towel to my face when my boyfriend came home from work. He asked what had happened, and when I told him a car battery had fallen on my face he just said, reasonably, that we did not have a car. Doing the school run with a big black eye the next day, I told the other mums, "It's not what you think", to which they were quick to reply, "We don't think anything!" (Much later, when I was to have frequent accidents in blackout, waking up with something bruised, cut, broken or burned, I tried to claim adult onset dyspraxia, but as my fumy breath generally entered the room before my broken body did, nobody believed a word of it.)

Then I got mugged, when I was with the children, in a local natural beauty spot, which was also, fittingly, a cemetery. There was no place I felt more at ease than with dead people whose deaths had not affected me directly. My boyfriend had run the London marathon that day, and all of us were in high spirits. The children and I went to the shops to get things to bake a celebration cake for him. We took our normal route through the cemetery, which was sunny and crowded and full of the usual professional dog walkers, cruising gay guys and families, like us, just enjoying the sunlight dappling through the trees. At some point the children were slightly ahead of me, and two guys approached me from behind, one covering my mouth with his sweaty palm, the other trying to grab my handbag. "Don't scream," said the one with his hand over my mouth. For a second he took his hand off my mouth, to help the other guy get my bag off my shoulder. I screamed, and the children looked back at me, taking the scene in, watching the creeps try to drag me behind one of the bigger headstones.

To be mugged, not particularly violently, is to me almost an inevitable part of urban life. But being mugged in front of my kids was a new level of wrong. They tugged at the bag until the strap broke and the contents – keys, pills, money and wet wipes – were scattered over the ground. The guys ran off, not taking anything. The kids were hiding behind the legendary stone carving of the Bostock Lion, a sculpture meant to bring good fortune to those who whisper in its ear and rub its nose.

Someone had called the cops, and we did the obligatory drive round in the cop car, trying to spot the muggers, but my daughter was getting carsick, and the whole task just felt pointless. One cop said, "I am a parent and I would NEVER cut through that cemetery. It just isn't safe." Except it had been safe up until then, and he seemed to be having a pop at my parenting judgment. Back home, my boyfriend eventually turned up, red-faced, stiff-legged, triumphant, and said he had completed the marathon. We all clambered to tell him our own versions of our mugging hell, not only taking the wind out of his sails, but hijacking what should have been a celebratory day, and making it into a drama.

Later that year – partially to try to unjinx what had felt like a particularly bad one – we got married. We had a great knees-up afterwards, with all our musical friends getting up to do a song. I used to judge how good a party was according to whether a drunk woman who was NOT ME, had lost one or both of her shoes. I don't know how women lose shoes. It's a thing that really drunk women do. Many years later, in rehab, I would say to my key-worker, "But I never, ever lost my shoes," as if it were a significant marker as to how out of control you were. So when I saw a woman traipsing out of the bar at our wedding, shoeless, I thought, "Result! Good Omen. Our marriage will last for ever. Way longer than her shoes."

My son, who had been "no trouble" until this point, started to get extremely anxious if I were late for the school pick-up. His teacher told me that he told her he was afraid that "bad men were going to take his mummy away". We decided to use a bit of magical thinking to combat the mugging hangover. As a family, we returned to the Bostock Lion, each of us whispering for something special. My son, whose newly restored hearing made it hard for him to modulate his voice from normal speaking to whisper, asked the lion to crumble into lots of bits of stone and cover him up. He was only six, and wanted to be buried in stone. Now I had two anxious children, and lacked the can-do, mustn't-grumble, no-nonsense, dust-ourselves-down attitude that saw other families through minor crises. It was just another molehill to turn into a mountain, and another excuse to up my dosage. I sought help from the Child and Adolescent Mental Health Services in our borough, trying to fix my kids without making any meaningful attempt to fix myself.

I was spending more time at home getting quietly out of it. The husband off to work, the children off to school, me, ostensibly, sending feature ideas to editors of magazines: *Ten Ways to Beat Stress, Ten Ways to Beat Cravings, Lose Ten Pounds in Ten Days.* My writing life was eked out in features involving ten of everything. My drug life was punctuated by ten milligrams at regular intervals.

Were there other mums in my situation? Sure they joked about "wine o' clock", but I could not bring myself to ask if it was normal to drink neat spirits while making family dinner. Is Neem oil really the go-to treatment for nits? Do your kids eat five a day? Do you think Tony Blair might be lying? Do you know a good maths tutor? When is it too early to start drinking?

Cleaning, London 2015
THE TIDY BACHELOR

TOWER BLOCK, HIGH UP. TWO bedrooms. Very clean inside, though filthy windows. Bachelor, divorced, or gay. No female touches. A collection (eBay, I suspect) of toys from his 70s childhood – enough to merit collection status but not so many to qualify as eccentric, excessive or trapped in the past. I survey the flat and yearn for this tidy, uncomplicated life, imagining his joy as he loosens his tie when he comes in from work, and sees a note from a neighbour, that they have collected a parcel for him. Another toy to add to his nostalgic collection.

He has a booze cabinet. The latest coffee-maker. Lots of books in the bathrooms about quirky bits of London and "crap towns". Shirts that need very careful pressing. An out-of-tune, I suspect rarely played, guitar. Lots of framed pictures leaning against the wall, waiting to be hung. Evidence of lots of business or pleasure trips. Partially packed or unpacked bags. Flight itineraries. Furniture he probably refers to as "pieces". A tidy, organised life uncluttered by other people or a family. Part of me is so in love with this flat, the balance between the past and the present, that I try to figure out if I can change the locks and just squat there, starting my new life as a hard-working bachelor whose only visible vice is collecting old toys. I know another guy who does this, toy collecting, and he volunteers for the Samaritans, which makes me presume that this guy does too. Which makes him a saint as well. Sometimes it is not enough to clean a flat; sometimes I just want to start life all over again, as this person whose flat I am cleaning, based on the most spurious evidence.

I want to get this clean right, because, while I cannot BE him, I still want to visit his flat weekly and make it nicer than it is already. It is an easy gig, and I always finish before the allotted time. I I love ironing his shirts with the special scented ironing water. His toys seem to be in ascending order of year and popularity. His *Rough Guides* are geographically ordered. My trouble is this: if you put things back in the exact right place, it looks as though you didn't lift them to dust underneath. Put the toys in slightly the wrong order and he will know you've moved them to clean underneath, but will he be annoyed if you put them back in the wrong place? Did I put his collection of Six Million Dollar Man toys back in chronological order after I dusted them? Did he notice that the feather duster I banged on his balcony took a swan dive to the tenth floor, its blue feathered arse sticking out of a lower railing, never to be retrieved? Could I live with a well-stocked booze cabinet? No, even though I have been off the drink for a few years, the temptation would be too great. I imagine myself pissed, playing with the Six Million Dollar Men, throwing them off the balcony, to see if they could fly. I can't even remember why I stopped doing this job. It was too nice, too easy, and I didn't deserve it.

Chapter Sixteen

When Zach died, I began to feel what I can only describe as inappropriately devastated. As if I did not have enough shit going on, on the estate, to preoccupy my sad magnet mind. I had developed a talent for sadness, for pathological empathy. I felt I needed a ringside seat to see what other families did when one of their number was taken out suddenly, in Zach's case, on a five-a-side football pitch. Part of it was psychological forensics: I wanted to see how another family coped, as it was dawning on me that perhaps my own family did not do grief in the textbook way. I couldn't say my family had got it wrong... I expect my own mother acted on the advice of well-meaning friends and doctors. Stay strong, stay medicated, as needed. But now I was grown up myself, I needed to see if there was some other, better way. I just wasn't curious enough to stay off drugs in order to find out what was and was not OK in the realm of other people's losses.

Not only did I feel other people's pain, I believed I felt their pain more strongly than they did. I was a grief thief, appropriating other people's tragic events and magnifying them to the extent that in my mind, it justified the necessity of more sedation. I was turning into a cyber pharmaceutical fanatic. I started to get a series of good batches of drugs from Romania. Nobody gets good internet drugs from Romania. It never occurred to me that, even when they were not from Romania but some other Eastern European country, the fake prescription sheet would always be the same. Dr S. Merk. Dr Smirk. Smirk away, I thought, just send me drugs that work, Smerk.

I started getting strange phone calls from underwater-sounding foreign voices, telling me if I ordered twice the amount of X, they would throw in 50 erectile-dysfunction drugs for free. I remember sitting with my mobile, perched on the end of a sandpit my kids were playing in and shouting down the line, in front of all the other hot and sandy mums and kids, "NO, I DO NOT NEED ERECTILE DYSFUNCTION DRUGS, THAT PART IS ALL HUNKY DORY. IF YOU ARE GOING TO THROW IN EXTRA, SEND MORE VALIUM!" Some of the other mums and one of the dads looked over at me, half curious, half aghast. Yeah, yeah. I was past caring what other people thought. It didn't help that I used to sit at the edge of the sandpit, in my faded posh jumble sale Boden skirt, reading *American Psycho*.

I played a lot with Google, a search engine Paul had showed me, and was able to find a connection to Buzzy, my old pal and fellow Valium-muncher from NYC. Through a series of emails and contacting friends of friends, I learned that Buzzy had died some years ago, and that my first boyfriend's brother had died as well. I was not sure how sad I was allowed to be. I had not seen either of them in over ten years. I wrote an article about it and called it "Google Grief".

Google it. My name will come up.

When I started telling people about my old friend Buzzy who had died, I would get the look, the look that says, yeah, so? And maybe: "How did he die, how old was he?" But I didn't know either of these things. I did know the conversational currency of death-related and distressing news coming from me was starting to wear thin. When a good friend told me she had chucked her adoring and wonderful husband, I cried as if I were that husband. Looking more stricken than she was, I whispered, "You won't always feel this bad..." and she said, "I don't think I feel as bad as you do."

It was a conversational tic of my mother's as well. She might ring me and say, in an ominous and breaking-bad-news sort of voice, "You remember Jerry, from apartment 3C, worked in real estate, moved to Long Island, adopted that kid, the cute one who did ballet?"

"No, Ma, doesn't ring a bell."

"Yeah you do, he gave the best Halloween candy, always wrapped, Tootsie Rolls, I think. His wife had a wig. Not from cancer, just one of those nice wigs that... Yes, you know him, you just forgot. His sister had an apartment in Richmond Hill. You went to second grade with her daughter..."

"No. No recollection."

"...who had pet turtles, you bugged me for a turtle..."

"No, what, Ma? What about him?"

"He died."

And while these exchanges struck me as comical, I was doing pretty much the same thing, seriously.

I was the life and soul of any break-up, terminal illness or sudden death. I rang a hospital ward, where a girlfriend of a friend of mine was having some sort of surgical procedure, complicated by the fact that she had a rare allergy to anaesthetic. I knew her name and the procedure she was having but, in terms of being a proper friend to her, we were the sort of people who would nod to each other and maybe air-kiss at social gatherings. I was very much not on the front line of her drama, and yet that is where I felt most at home, in the ringside seat of other people's misery.

"Are you a relation to the person in question?" asked the hospital receptionist.

"Not exactly but my good friend..."

And I could hear my mother's voice in my own, talking about wigs and Tootsie Rolls and death.

I became an expert at nodding gravely. A nod that said, let me know if you need any help, if you need someone who you don't know very well, or maybe even don't like very much, to sob uncontrollably when the procedure does not work and to ring all your friends and relations to put them on a rota of making you food and driving you to appointments or sitting with you in the hospice, if, like, it comes to a hospice. Which I am sure it won't. I can say a lot in a grave nod.

When a mum friend told me her sister had cancer, I went home and cried my eyes out as if it were my sister. At the funeral of this friend's sister, I went up to one of her sons, a teenager lost in a sea of hair dye and mixed feelings, and said something that comes straight out of a

badly scripted made-for-TV movie: "I'm here for you."
He stared at me blankly. I handed him my number on a
torn strip of mayonnaise-stained napkin.

The kid said, "I don't mean to be rude, but I don't
actually know who you are." And at that moment, dosed
up on Romanian Valium and vodka from a secret flask,
neither did I.

My daughter's friend's mother's mother, whom I had
never met, died after a brief illness. I knew my daughter's friend's mother well enough, but was hardly a first-
response sort of friend. Not that this deterred me from
showing up, when her mother died, on her doorstep, with
a present, a jar of blackcurrant jam for diabetics, though
she is not diabetic; it was the first thing that caught my
eye in the corner shop, after I had bought my Smirnoff.
She opened the door, puffy-faced from crying, still in her
bathrobe. I said, "I heard…" and, pulling the jar of jam
out of my bag, added "Here, have this." I was immediately
appalled at how crap these words were, how inadequate.
She looked puzzled, but took the jam, and we stood there
on the doorstep, both of us shivering, her from shock,
me from some sort of nascent forerunner of the DTs. She
said, "If you don't mind, I would really like to be on my
own right now."

Determined to keep the conversation going at all costs,
I said, "Is there anyone I can call for you?", like a sombre
liaison officer from the homicide squad. As if she did not
have a telephone herself.

It is weird, this attraction to deep grief. It seems so
familiar to me, even if I hardly know the people involved

all that well. Let me mop up your emotional shit. Better still, give it to me, so I can amplify it and take it all on myself. Meanwhile, the people themselves, the primary grievers or sufferers, seemed to crack on with life, with families, with this new knowledge that life was short, and best to live it to its fullest, not to forget the dead but to honour them, for who, if they truly love us, ever wants to see us forever sad? Not the living. Not the dead.

As death and drugs started to prise me away from my own busy family, housework felt unimportant. It took an effort I was not willing to extend to anything as banal and workaday as a clean house. I was the opposite of house proud: more slut proud, proud that my mind was on Higher Things. Or, I was just too high to care. My own housekeeping skills were haphazard and slovenly. I might clean something if I remembered that it was dirty, or I might see the dirt and then forget it, to think about more important stuff, like death and drugs.

When I started cleaning houses to make money, after I had got sober, I did not like to see the things that looked like those that were once in my house. Because they reminded me that I should have cleaned my own house, or that I should be cleaning my own house now, except it was no longer my house. All of this STUFF families buy… it all needs to be tidied away, or cleaned, or replaced. But these are THINGS. I tidied MYSELF right out of my family's life and, in cleaning houses that looked like the one I left, I found myself asking big questions to which I had no reasonable answer. Why did I leave them? When you are sober, everything is very clear, except one lingering question: why did I do that SHIT? Why did I fuck up something so good? So now I am the hired wife of the wife, picking up their stuff, cleaning their things, as they work, or spend quality time with their kids. I am unqualified to do quality time. But I can pick up the trail of toys going up the stairs. Every happy family has the same mess: the abandoned browning slices of banana smeared across the plastic table of a high chair; the Lakeland-catalogue kitchen gadgets to make funfair food at home, so you don't actually have to go to the funfair – a candy floss maker, a waffle iron, a popcorn machine. These were the early days of the middle-class march against junk food and sugar, before the quinoa-sie grabbed all the Jaffa cakes out of grubby fingers and replaced them with rice cakes. Handcrafted wooden toys, sold at artisan toy shops. No, no resemblance there, at least. I loved cheap plastic and noise, just as my kids did. At Christmas I bought them the noisiest toys: keyboard sets, drum kits, computer-type toys that made lots of repetitive electronic beeps. Drove other grown-ups crazy, but not me. I loved the noise of my kids on a sugar high. It was evidence, but not really proof, that there was life and fun in my family, despite the quiet, sedated life I was slipping into, as this shop-bought chaos turned our flat into a nerve-jangling wall of kiddie sounds.

Cleaning, London 2015
THE FAMILY AT HALF-TERM

IT IS HALF-TERM BREAK. THE father is decorating or pretending to. Actually he is listening to the cricket and yelping "yes!" or "noooo" at various intervals, while trying to wallpaper the front room. The mother is readying her girls, aged about three and five, for a trip to see some family. The wife explains everything in a hurry, while trying to micromanage the departure of the girls. Toys to occupy them on the train journey. Snacks (carrot batons, cherry tomatoes, rice cakes and hummus, all packed in those hard-to-open-and-close, clicky-clacky containers). The girls sit patiently while mum applies sun cream to every exposed inch of them. To me, she says, "Just the usual: dust, vacuum, straighten things out, the bath is a bit of a state, but don't scrub too hard as it will scratch it." And they leave, gaily, the mum grabbing a pink plastic potty almost as an afterthought as they go out of the door.

It is a tall narrow house, a couple of sizable rooms on every floor. Bathroom as big as a bedroom. Nautical theme, washed out on purpose, light-blue paint, seashells everywhere, a ropey bathmat, bits of stone and driftwood lovingly placed around the room. Chipped, off-white paint on the floorboards. An antique railway sign for a seaside destination, fare written in old money. I scrub, but not too hard, at the beautiful, claw-footed bath. I pick up things that need picking up along the stairs, depositing things where I think they belong: Kumon maths books in the girls' shared bedroom, a White Company brochure next to the wife's side of the bed. A Jamie Oliver cookery book in the kitchen. A bucket and spade in the small garden off the kitchen. It is a house of happy chaos, nothing exactly where it should be and, even after I have tidied, I know it will not stay this way for long. Child handprints below the bannisters. Jars of homemade jam with a red-and-white cloth covering the lid, and labels like "Sophie's gooseberry conserve" or "Molly's brambletastic spread". She belongs to some jam circle of hell where everyone gives everyone else a jar of excess jam. I hear the dad yelp with cricket-related glee or despair, as I finally reach the shockingly pristine parental bedroom, at the very top of the house, and I feel a longing, almost like a physical pain, somewhere around the womb area, now barren, now menopausal. I have to bend over, the way they tell you to when you've got cramp in your side.

I remember those excursions, those last-minute-by-the-door grabs (change of clothes for my daughter, usually, who suffered from carsickness). I remember my husband stopping the car at my daughter's weeping request and him taking her in his arms and putting her over his shoulder, where she was sick all down his back, and him saying so tenderly, "It's OK, you'll feel better now" – my son in the back, sleeping, or sipping from his spouted cup. It was my life once, it was my outside life and it looked pretty normal. I remember at times, sitting at the kitchen table, playing some board game "suitable for all ages", and being a little bit bored, but also thinking, "These are the good days. Jam and family trips and family games. I have a family. I am the mother. This is the life I wanted to make." A sort of domestic tranquillity, except, in my case, this elusive domestic tranquillity was to be shattered by tranquilliser abuse.

When I leave the house, I say to the father, who is still working (or not) on the same strip of wallpaper as he had been when I started the job four hours ago, "This is the good bit." And he says, "What? What's the good bit?" And I say, "Your life, right now. This is the good bit."

A wack-job thing to say, totally out of context. He smiles nervously. "Riiight…"

I can risk the wack-job comment as it is a one-off clean – their regular housekeeper is on holiday. It won't enrich his life or tell him anything he does not already know. But I can leave this job knowing that not only have I picked up all the stray Lego, but also I have given him the wisdom of… someone who did not know a good thing when she had it.

Chapter Seventeen

Rita was my mother's sister, the eldest of three children and the one who never quite got away. My uncle and my mother both got married and moved away, not only from Liverpool but also from England. Rita got a job in a chemist's, helping dispense the sort of drugs that I craved. Her life was one of routine and, I imagine, great blocks of boredom, which she broke up by visiting friends and relations in other countries. As her parents, my grandparents, got older and frailer, she stopped working at the chemist's and became a full-time carer. It was an exhausting, thankless task and she was confined to the house for long periods of time, escaping in her beloved Mills and Boon doctor–nurse romance novels in her bedroom at night, with the twin candlewick bedspreads and the hot-water bottle put in the bed hours before she retired.

She never spoke of men or romance, though she had a thing for one of the Three Tenors, a girlish crush that was both endearing and slightly disturbing, in that it seemed to displace any possibility of a real-life, attainable crush. She was also forever on a diet, sprinkling coarse wheat bran over everything she ate, to speed the passage and possibly dodge the calorific absorption of any food that passed her lips. She had a voluptuous hourglass figure, and an array of corsets and hefty underwear to keep everything in.

When my grandparents died, a few years apart, she gained a new freedom. She sold the family house to move into an assisted-living flat, which she adored – getting new furniture, carpets everywhere, having the heating on as high as she wanted. Then she got sick. First, a pain in her side, which later moved to her middle, and then all over. She was diagnosed with cancer and my cousin's wife looked after her devotedly. I was down in London, with my husband and children and drugs and, when the end was near, my cousin called and said he had some bad news. I took this to mean she had died. So I rang my mother in the States and she rang everyone else in the States who knew and loved Rita. Then I rang my cousin again and it transpired that Rita was not actually dead, but dying. The one thing I was REALLY GOOD at doing, ringing people and solemnly announcing death, I had fucked up. This was me all over. Jumping the death gun. The over-reportage, the over-feeling of death. Getting things a bit wrong, or very wrong. I had to ring my mother again, to tell her that Rita was not exactly dead yet, but that her death was imminent, so it might be best not to ring everyone to tell them that she hadn't gone yet, but would have in a day or two. My mother considered this and laughed a bleak laugh, and said, "You know, trust you... Someone is dead or alive." And I told her about my cousin's open-ended understatement, meaning the end was nigh, but not there yet. What did it matter anyway?

There is a huge spectrum between life and death. I thought my mother would know better than most what it was like to live on the death end of life. She fought cancer. Twice. But really, really, it always seemed to me that her life was time to kill, as Caitlin Thomas, Dylan Thomas's widow put it, a leftover life to kill. Time to kill before Caitlin was reunited with Dylan, time to kill before my mother was entombed, somewhere in Montreal, with her Sid.

They talk about the half-life of drugs, which means how long it takes all traces of it to leave your body. Valium has a very long half-life, even though the effect of the drug is pretty short. But the phrase is fitting, for when you are addicted you are barely living any life at all. I know the spectrum of life and death thing, like my mother, only through different channels.

And there is another half-life, in getting clean and sober. First, you get off the drugs and drink. Then, you have to figure out how to live life without drugs and drink, because even if you have done this before, you will have forgotten. There are programmes that give you a plan. But if you don't follow it, as I didn't, you will not know how to do life without doing drugs. So you will do them again.

Cleaning, London 2015
BURNT OFFERINGS: THE RELAPSE CLEAN

I AM ON MY WAY to a house-share clean in Stepney after getting drunk and hideously burned the night before. I think I can still cook, in high heels, loaded. I think I can still get loaded, despite two years of sobriety. I wake up, having swaddled myself and my burns, clumsily, in bandages.

There is usually only one person in the house when I get there, a softly spoken Irish woman in some field of academia. I arrive at the clean and realise the bits of bandage that are not stuck to the broken-blister burns are unravelling. I look like a hungover cast-off from a bad episode of *Scooby Doo* – the Mummy Maid – except, instead of chasing those meddling kids through an abandoned fairground, I am pushing an ineffectual Hoover around some badly stained carpets and wincing every time I have to move anything. There is a queer smell in the house, a rotting smell that I'd never noticed before. Perhaps it had always been there but masked by cooking smells.

The Irish woman stops at her door and says, "Do ya think you can have a quick go at my room, just a wee bit of hoovering and a light dusting?"

"Sure," I say, unsteadily. "Thing is, do you smell that, um, smell?"

She sniffs showily, noisily. "Sure, there is a bit of a pong but I didn't really notice it before. Hey, look, you're losing something from your, um, trousers, a bandage or something?"

I can see I am trailing the bandage, bits of it bloody or smeared with pus. I can also see that the smell of decay is coming from me, from the bandages.

I sit down heavily at the top of the stairs. "I think I am not very well."

The Irish woman brings me into her room and she does a Google search for the nearest hospital, which is the London Hospital. She suggests I make my way there.

In the waiting room I think about all the AA meetings I have been to since coming out of rehab, all the times I have said, "Came to believe a power greater than ourselves could restore us to sanity" but not really felt it.

I sit in the chair with my A and E ticket number, waiting for them to call me in for the stagger of shame down the corridor, to lie to some triage nurse about how I came to be so badly burnt.

After a four-hour wait, the nurse who sees me tells me in no uncertain terms that they do not change bandages in A and E and that I am to go to a walk-in clinic which is much further away.

On the Tube to the walk-in centre, the smell coming off me is making people back away. This is all wrong. I am supposed to make things smell nice. I sit down in another orange plastic chair, shifting my weight from side to side to find a way of sitting that hurts less.

The nurse does my bandages briskly, humming a tune I recognise from the church I have been attending sporadically.

I stop cleaning for a few weeks after that, to let the burns heal up. I stop drinking. Again. I start going to recovery meetings most nights, trying very hard to believe that this power, God, whoever, whatever, will keep me from picking up the next drink.

Chapter Eighteen

About a year after Rita died, my friend Lizzy had a baby, and after she had the baby, the bump was replaced by a lump.

She got really sick, really quickly, but remained dignified and positive. Her lovely husband Tim did all the right stuff. Being a hard worker, being a great dad, being a loyal partner, all the while staying on some sort of form. High functioning. He took her to doctors, oncologists, the dirty realists. He did the right thing, always. Then the doctor said, there is nothing more we can do. It's too aggressive. I think they were the last to leave the clinic that night. It was a long time and a lot of drugs ago so I can't remember the story exactly, but I do remember the part that they were the last to leave the clinic, as it was getting dark. And it was getting dark in every way possible. When I was told this story, it all got jumbled up. I felt his pain. I felt her pain. I felt the perhaps mechanical bad-news pain of the doctor's delivery. I was the patient, the husband of the patient, the doctor, even the kid. I was all these people going through all this awfulness and feeling it magnified. The psycho-empath.

Of course, every drug addict will make every bad event all about himself or herself. And every bad event is another reason to take more drugs. I pictured the forlorn couple, my friends, going through the revolving door, maybe not bothering with the anti-bac gel on the way out, thinking, "We are beyond bacteria, we are now in the world of palliative care." At this point I started to talk to God. Out loud. At my bar. We had got another home bar at some point, looking to replicate the silliness of the one in our rented rooms. Only that first bar, in the rented place, had only ever been a joke. This bar was for serious drinking. The centrepiece of big, mad noisy parties we threw, but also, for my own private drinking pleasure.

Sometimes I was the bartender and sometimes I was the sozzled customer, but I would pack my kids off to school, go down to my bar, start drinking and telling God, you know, this is just not ON. If you save Lizzy I will stop drinking. I will be a nicer mum. If you spare this one, I will stop being a fuck-up.

It was a strange thing to do, drinking spirits and getting spiritual. I wanted to cover myself on all bases. I started to go to the church Lizzy went to, even though I was not even Church of England, or any sort of Christian. I was Jewish but a bad Jew. I didn't follow any practices. I didn't understand much at all about my own religion. I just knew about the death side, of course. When someone dies, they have to be buried really fast. The bereaved cover up all reflective surfaces so they can't look at themselves, which I think is a good thing. People bring food. People sit on tiny chairs for several days, to think about the dead person, and after those days are over, you get on with life. It's a good plan, but it was not my plan. It was not my mother's plan. They don't go on much, if at all, about an afterlife.

Neither did Lizzy's church, but there was a sense of warmth and conviviality there, and sometimes they talked about heaven but it was not the main thing. They did heaven, but only parenthetically. I found the services confusing at first, not only because I was half-cut most of the time, but because they gave you so many pieces of paper – the hymn book, the order of service, the mass card – and people would switch from one to the other, automatically knowing what to do, and I would just sit in the back and kneel on the little embroidered cushion and pray: "God, please save my friend Lizzy."

Then the money from Rita's will came through. It was enough to fly me and my family to New York and Boston, even to stay in a hotel. We would have a really nice trip to the States and I would try to be sober. I told Lizzy, you gotta hang on because I am going to bring you all that cornball tourist stuff from New York, a snow-storm globe with the Empire State Building in it, an "I HEART NY" t-shirt, something with butterflies because I know you love butterflies.

Lizzy deteriorated rapidly when we were in New York. More pills, visits from the hospice nurses and vicars, a wound in her leg, caused by a brush with a bramble, that never healed. The last night of our trip, we got a call: now Lizzy was in the hospice and it would not be long.

We flew back and went to the hospice. The lovely vicar from the church was there. Lizzy was breathing noisily and her mother was saying, "It's OK, sweetheart, you can go now." And I was like, "No, you can't go, not yet, you need to see your snowstorm and the butterflies and stuff. You need to see your beautiful daughter grow up." As if she hadn't thought of that, as if that very thought had not caused her as much pain as the cancer itself. The immense stupidity of my last words to her washes over me in waves of hot shame, still. Not for the first time, not for the last time, I should have just shut up. The only comforting thought is that she didn't hear any of it anyway.

Somewhere during this time, or just before this time, there was a healing mass at the church and I said a prayer for Lizzy and the nice vicar, who spoke to me later and said, "Sometimes God does not answer in the way we want him to." Well that was surely the truth. Lizzy had died. Life was becoming desperately unfun. We stopped throwing our big, mad parties. It was not that I couldn't cope with the hangovers. I could not cope with being sober at all.

Cleaning, London 2015
THE PARTY'S OVER

ONE OF THE OFFICE CLEAN workers has had a party. I mean, a party to end all parties. Could I clean up the morning after? Well, sure, I love this stuff. I love evidence of a night of partying. I can't party any more. I have forgotten how to have fun, sober. But I can be of service. There is always a crying-confused girl I can mother. Lost her knickers, sick in her own hair. "Where am I? What did I do?" Aw Christ, she will say, she is giving up drinking.

She dances with a guy who lives there. He's got his knee in her groin and she is up for it. They shout at each other over the bass and drums: GREAT PARTY, INNIT? YAH! TUNE!

And maybe they do lines of coke and stay up all night together instead of having sex. They might lie side by side, exhausted; she may get up to pee and notice he snores and drools and his room is a tip, and actually he's not all that attractive. So she slips her clothes on quietly, orders an Uber and gets the hell out of there to have the rest of her hangover in her tiny room in her shared flat.

I find the address, on a sign-less side street, by following a trail of puddles of sick. After pounding on the steel-reinforced door, I am let in by a guy wearing a towel around his middle, and he gestures widely at the mess. He points to a roll of bin bags, some cleaning fluids, sponges and a mop. "That's the stuff. I need to lie down now."

"You do that, poppet."

Poppet? I have never called anyone that in my life. Other people's hangovers make me weirdly maternal and overly friendly.

There is not one surface of the enormous flat not covered in spilt something. Not one tray of food not only uneaten but also not used as a makeshift ashtray. Particularly hummus. Hummus is the serious partier's ashtray.

I have a method, which is to first gather up all the trash, all the empties, all the uneaten but clearly off or fag-ended leftovers and stuff it all into bin bags. Each room reveals a fresh hell of trash, and then French doors leading to a garden area reveal a worse collection. Burgers abandoned on the barbie. Tubs of congealed dips dotted along a water feature, also littered with fag ends.

I am cleaning and feel so clean. I have not done these drugs that took away the appetite. I have not drunk this beer, this punch, these litres of spirits. I am the one putting things back in order. Now and then a girl wearing a boy's t-shirt runs in the general direction of the toilets, one hand covering her mouth, the other gripping her stomach. All the girls, not that many but enough to notice a pattern, are model-pretty and model-skinny, but look very different from the way they look in magazines. After a few minutes they emerge, wan and pale. One comes up to me and whispers in sicky breath, "Where am I?"

Oh great! I can be a mum. For a minute, I can be a mum again.

Michele Kirsch

"You are in the East End. There was a party here last night."

"Shit. I live in Notting Hill." And a fresh spasm of nausea hits her and she runs back to the loos. She comes back and I hand her a wet wipe. Actually it is a Dettol wet wipe, for surfaces, but she takes it gratefully. Then I get her some water and sit quietly with her. She is trying to piece together the night before. Instinctively, I rub her back. She shoots me a "Whhoooa, what's all this" look.

I remove my hand. In sobriety, I sometimes take the surrogate mum thing too far.

The party is clearly over. For her. For me. For the people who got so loaded they just won't remember any fun they had, if they did have fun.

Everybody will lie and say what a great time they had. I will have tidied up, and stolen a lost mummy moment with a strange girl.

Chapter Nineteen

Around about this time, as I was starting to go to church, finding my writing work tapering off, and losing interest in domestic matters, my daughter's anxiety attacks were getting worse. She would go to school and run out of classes, or not go to school at all. And I knew how awful it felt, that gripping, needless fear, that fear of fear, and yet I was not in a great position to help her out. I had hoped that, by breeding with a calm and gentle guy, I would somehow breed out the anxiety, that my kids would not suffer the way I did. My son seemed to carry on in a normal fashion, going to school, not much interested in it but getting there and staying there. But my girl, she suffered. She woke up with fear and it gripped her all day, most days.

We took her to therapy. She had special counsellors at school but they didn't really get it. They thought she was just being naughty, playing truant. They used to ring, or email, and say: "We don't know what to do about your kid." I didn't know either. I didn't know how to help her. In fact, what I did was the opposite of help her. I shouted at her; I said, "Look, this anxiety thing, it snowballs, you stop going to class, you stop going to school, you stop going out. You just have to go in and plant your bum on the seat. If you can't concentrate, that's OK, you can catch up at home, but you have to go to school, or you will just stop." I was horrible to her. I thought I could make it so unbearable at home that school would look good in comparison but that was an unkind and unhelpful ploy.

Home for her became this place where mum shouted at her. She was eating into my alone time and drinking time. I gave her the standard advice for anxiety – just do it – but I knew in my heart she could not. I could not, not without drugs. But I wasn't going to let HER know that. I knew she would not take that hard advice, as I had not when I was young, when I used to run out of classes, or, in the medicated years, stumble out of them. The irony was, as part of my new-found Christianity, I had to do service and reach out to the wider community. Help fractured families in trouble, while ignoring my own, which was falling apart at the seams. At least, my seams. I volunteered at a family contact centre, where estranged dads met up with their kids once a week for a few hours, to play in a supervised setting. The contact centre was in the basement of the church. We would sign the dads in, and the mums would go for coffee upstairs, in case the child did not want to see the father. We always had kids running back up the stairs, in tears. The fathers often didn't know how to play with the kids. They spent the time texting, or looking bored, or letting the kid play games on their phone. Meanwhile the mothers would sit in tiny nursery seats upstairs, with their infants, the second babies, and bitch about the dads. Many of the marriages had been arranged, and the husbands beat them. It was a voluntary position I was entirely unsuited for, not only unable to help these broken families, but doing a pretty good job of messing up my own. There was a lift for wheelchair users and I remember being able to down a mini bottle of Absolut in the time it took it to get from the basement to the ground floor, or the ground floor to the basement. When it hit my empty stomach, I would emerge from the lift feeling not so bad about everything. If I were travelling downstairs, I might saunter over to an uninterested father and say, "Hey, would you like to play a game with your kid? Maybe read them a story, or do some colouring?" We were not really supposed to interact with the dads but the booze made me bold, in a what-the-heck, they-can't-sack-me, I'm-a-volunteer sort of way.

On the walk home, I was filled with a new spirit of love and compassion for my daughter, my husband, my son. At least we were intact for the time being. He was a great dad. She was suffering, a kind of suffering I knew and understood. My son retreated into whatever took his interest at the time. Soldiers. Elvis. Batman. Arsenal. But slowly I was retreating from them, the bar having a greater pull, making fewer demands on my time, on my patience, on anything. By the time I went up the stairs to my home, I needed topping up. If my daughter was still in bed, trying to put off facing the terrors of the day, I would start to shout. "You've got to get out of that bed. You've got to try, or you'll wind up agoraphobic, unable to go anywhere! Is that what you want?" Within the space of a fifteen-minute walk, I turned from a mild, gently encouraging Christian woman into the bitch from hell. The fear that gripped her gripped me too, only I had pills and vodka to blur the edges of panic. She had, what? A crazed mother, unable to express the compassion and empathy I so readily gave away, albeit drunkenly, at the contact centre.

On the walk to church or the contact centre, I would go down this little road, and there was this one house always for rent. It was the smallest house I had ever seen, one room downstairs, and one room upstairs. The houses either side of it had been knocked down, so it was exposed on all sides. I was dying to look inside to see if it was as small as it looked from the outside. I took to standing outside it, trying to peer in the windows. I had a flask for the vodka by then. I would stand outside the house and take sips from the flask, until it was empty. Drinking vodka and staring at a house. It was as mindless as shovelling popcorn in your mouth at the movies. Could I afford to rent it? I desperately wanted it. I wanted to run away, only I didn't really see it like that. I just wanted a little place to not have to do anything.

One day I was walking down the road with my friend Helen and we stopped at the house and I said, "I really have a crush on this house. I want to live here one day." I didn't say, "one day soon", like, tomorrow – just "one day". And she looked at me quizzically and asked, "But what about your husband, your children?" and I thought, yeah, what about them? But I could not say this, it was too awful. Mums were not supposed to run away from home. That was the kid's job. So I back-peddled and said, "Oh, I don't mean now, I mean in the future, just a little place near church, near the shops, near my volunteer work. No immediate neighbours, so I can play my records really loud, if I want to."

It was the point in my drinking where it was not about one for the road; it was about one for the road, one for the pavement, one for the walk home, and then as many as I needed, at home, at the home bar. At some point, almost any addiction story starts to sound the same as another. The substance may be different, the financial situation may be different, the degree of physical and emotional harm to oneself and others may be different, but what it really comes down to is that the addict stops "living to use, and starts using to live". This is where you can't kid yourself this is a rough patch, or towards the end of a sickly, hedonistic path, a very long-lost weekend that will end in tears. This is the point where as soon as you wake up, you want everyone, including, maybe especially, those you love most, to just go away, so you can use, or drink, or both. It vaguely occurred to me that something was not right, that my clothes were falling off me, that my children and husband were unhappy at best, scared for my life at worst. And at this point, it turned out that, I needed an operation on my foot. I had never had an operation before, so I had no notion of what to expect, apart from the fact that, at least for the duration of the operation and perhaps for some time afterwards, I could not drink or use drugs. And they would knock me out. I was looking forward to that bit.

I had the operation and, for a short while, I really

enjoyed my convalescence. I retreated to the spare room, receiving visitors, who brought me gossip, magazines, music, flowers. A friend brought cocktails, but even I knew these would make me ill or kill me if I combined them with the painkillers I was on. Paul and his American wife, with whom he had eventually been reunited, had narrowly escaped Hurricane Katrina in New Orleans and, facing an uncertain future, they'd come back to London. I was drifting in and out of sleep, but I remember we were talking enthusiastically about life after death after life. Paul was excited about something he was writing for a computer magazine. It was about how difficult it was to delete the social media accounts, Facebook and so on, of the dead, and the pain this caused for those left behind, unless people used the dead person's page as a medium to communicate with them in dead-people cyberspace. Facebook was where the living coexisted with the dead. Like the end of James Joyce's story "The Dead", where the snow falls over the living and the dead, Facebook made no distinctions. Birthdays were still celebrated. Drunken, middle-of-the-night posts were left by the bereaved: still missing you every day, you are still here with me... Paul loved this idea. He loved the impossibility of deletion. "We can all live forever!" he enthused. He was to die suddenly, a few months later.

I think of him, sitting on the edge of my bed, me high on painkillers, him a little high, but not that high, on cocktails, telling me stories that made me laugh and made my foot hurt even more, but I didn't care, because he was the best friend a girl could have. The sun was streaming through the window. A cat was perched on the window-sill. The kids two doors down were playing football in the garden. The woman right next door lumbered heavily into her garden, rubbing the small of her back. Heavily pregnant, barefoot, she picked up the garden hose and gave her rose bushes a cursory sprinkle. My foot was killing me, but life felt so very good. I started to feel drowsy, so Paul and my friend left me in a painkiller haze, magazines all over the bed, boxes of pills and empty cocktail glasses on the side table, the daylight fading into a cool, grey, spring evening.

When the day starts to fade and turn into night, this is my favourite time to clean.

Cleaning, London 2015
THE BOWLING GREEN

I AM GRATEFUL WHEN BEN, whose offices I clean, offers me another gig, to clean the new restaurant he is starting up in Finsbury Square, right over the underground car park, right next to the beautiful bowling green. The clean will be every week night: just mop the floors, do the toilets, cash in hand. Somehow no matter how much I work during the day, I never mind getting to Finsbury Square for closing time. I like the walk towards Old Street, turning left at the roundabout, watching all the office workers pour out of the buildings at normal times, five or six, heading for the pubs, or the buses, or the mini versions of supermarkets. It is towards the end of spring, before the start of summer, but it is getting lighter at night, and the light is beautiful, particularly on the bowling green. The green keeper, who also sets up the bowls games, is a guy around my age. He smells familiar. Drink. We have a friendly but meaningless chat most days; each day he promises me a free game of bowls, at some non-specified time in the future. He forgets that he told me the same thing yesterday and the day before. We both know it will never happen.

As I am fond of the time between Christmas and New Year, so I am fond of the time between work and play, or work and home. People shed a layer of formality, they stop being the thing that they think defines them, at parties, when people ask, "What do you do?" and they say, "I'm a reporter for Bloomberg" or, "I do social media for a bespoke handbag designer." They crack open a beer, or change into gym clothes, or pick up kids at an afterschool club, and for a short window of time, they are in between the time they are earning money and getting to the place that the money affords. I have no in-between time any more. I clean during the day. At night, I change out of my cleaning clothes, if I have time, and sit in a room full of other people who have fucked up their lives but are now just grateful for being clean and sober. If I find myself at a party, which is hardly ever, and people ask what I do, I say, "I am a cleaner" and they are interested for about two minutes, after which, their eyes glaze over. I used to say, "I am a journalist and mum" and then have the whole who-do-you-write-for conversation…and how old are your kids. Now I am of no interest except to the guy who maintains the bowling green. We watch people start games, and break out the Pimms, in the early-summer, early-evening fading sunshine.

The mopping itself is useless; the restaurant workers are still packing up and treading over the floor all the time. The loos are not used very often and not as hideous as some others. I am booked in for two hours but the job takes very little time, so I mop slowly. The coffee guy is cleaning down his station; maybe Ben will put some music on, or maybe there will be an office party getting set up. I like the feel of closing time. It is a collective thing: now the work ends, the fun or relaxation begins. But I can only watch, as I am still working.

I spend much of the clean staring at the young office workers on the bowling green. The women, in their office clothes and tights, or barefoot, beer or glass of wine in one hand. Little bursts of laughter coming from one section or another. From my angle, draped over my mop in the glass-walled restaurant, they look to be having the time of their lives. The sun still just warm enough for them to leave their suit jackets on the bench. Most are only a couple of years older than my own daughter, who has just started an office job in the area. For a moment, I want to crash the party, listen to what young people talk about, watch them punch the air if the ball they are rolling goes to the right spot, and cover their faces with their hands when the balls go on their own little path. The kitchen workers are now cracking open bottles of beer and counting up the day's takings. Ben is sitting at a table, doing something on his laptop. The office workers playing bowls are getting louder, refilling the wine glasses, opening more beers, the game itself being the least of it.

I want to kick my shoes off. How nice the grass would feel under my feet. How nice the fading sun looks, as I start my walk home, stopping for a takeaway coffee, and wondering if I could ring my daughter, to say breezily, "Hey, are you still in the area? Do you want to grab some dinner with your old ma?" But she hasn't spoken to me for nearly a year, so that isn't going to happen.

Chapter Twenty

It was very easy being an invalid, when the excruciating pain had passed and I could carry on a bit longer; life in bed, on painkillers, was so much easier than trying to find work, trying to keep the kids OK, trying to do normal life. I liked the non-routine, looking at magazines, listening to the radio, dozing, waking up and taking another pill. But eventually even I got bored. Soon I was shuffling about in a big grey walking boot, slowly, painfully, always lilting to one side, as if I was half-cut, when in fact I was enduring a brief period of sobriety. I was not going to mix painkillers with alcohol. I was not ready to do the full Judy Garland.

My daughter seemed a bit more settled in school – maybe therapy, maybe Mum being unnaturally quiet. My son, as usual, was "no trouble". Paul, his wife and I all got freelance gigs copywriting for a chain store that was putting its entire back catalogue online. One day I had to find about 50 ways to describe slight variations on the exact same bra and a hundred ways to describe a "colour block" skirt, which to me looked like wearing a flag as a sari, the way that hippies used to do at festivals – three bold stripes, A line, 100 per cent polyester. I wrote, "This skirt looks like the flag of a country called FUN!" and sent it over to Paul, who was sub-editing and formatting all the copy. Paul rang and said, "I'd like to speak to the president of FUN," and, "Kirschy, you are getting desperate. We can't run that, a country called 'Fun'. I mean, what are you on, and uh, have you got any left?"

The thing was, I was not on anything much. I had weaned myself off the painkillers, finding I had less stomach for drink, and was taking Valium as needed, which at that time, was not every day. Every day I sent the increasingly independent kids off to school, the husband off to work, and sat at my computer, staring at ten identical ugly tops, trying to say how lovely they were in ten different search-engine-optimisation-friendly terms. And I was foxed. It was very hard to be nice about these tops. The man-made fabric made you sweat like a pig. The lacy details at the top meant you had to buy a special bra. The colours were all pastel and awful. They were the bridesmaid dresses of tops.

I emailed Paul, "But, seriously, wouldn't you just shoot me, or your wife, if we were to wear these things?" He wrote back that this was not the point; we had to make people really want these tops. So we carried on, in this virtual word factory, sending emails to each other, writing in spreadsheets, feeling demoralized/demoralised, but demoralized/demoralised together.

Then, one day, very early in the morning, the phone rang. My husband answered it, and told me Paul was dead. Bizarrely, my first instinct was to tell Paul that there was a rumour that he was dead. That we'd better check Facebook.

My husband and I robotically threw on some clothes and walked over to Paul's flat. In front of the flat was a coroner's van and we saw two guys loading a body bag into it. Paul and his wife lived next door to a good friend of his and ours. There were already a bunch of people in the house next door. Paul's friends, pacing, smoking, crying. It was difficult to piece together the story. Some friends had tried to ring him the night before. He had not been seen walking his dogs that morning. No matter what, Paul always walked the dogs. His wife was in America, about to get the worst phone call of her life. And I was about to make the worst phone call of my life. It later emerged that Paul had died of a heart attack, but at that stage the only information I could get was that, when it became apparent that Paul was unreachable and that he had not taken the dogs out, the police were called. Another friend went into the flat with the police and found Paul crouched against a wall. The dogs were next to him. The friend tried to wake him, I believe, but the police knew he was dead. Our friend, with the great immediate practicality that bad news can inspire in some, took the dogs out for a walk.

I went upstairs to call his parents in Belfast. I am good at this, breaking bad news, or so I told myself, usually to justify the breaking of bad news. But I didn't want to break this bad news. It was too raw and, as soon as I dialled, I thought, I won't actually say it. I will hint at it. There was some part of me that thought all the evidence was faulty, that a guy who looked very like Paul had died in Paul's flat. His mum picked up the phone and I said,

"It's Michele." And his mum replied, "Oh Michele, it's very early, are you OK?", and I said no, not really, that I had some very bad news, the worst news. About Paul.

She said something to Bill, her husband.

I was lost for words and playing for time. "See, the thing is, he always walks the dogs, but this morning he didn't walk the dogs, because he couldn't. He couldn't walk the dogs."

She said she didn't understand. Was he ill? I said, maybe he had been ill but it was worse than being ill, what I had to tell her. I said, "You know he's so good about the dogs, he always walks the dogs, well, he can't walk them this morning, and he can't walk them tomorrow. He didn't walk the dogs."

She said very calmly, "Are you trying to tell me that Paul is dead?"

I said, "Yes, I think that is what I am trying to tell you, that Paul is dead. He couldn't walk the dogs. So the police came. And they found him. Someone else is walking the dogs."

Here she said something to her husband. Then I said I think I need to ring off now, but I will ring back when I find out more.

Desperate for something to do, I appointed myself the official bearer of bad news. I rang everyone but his wife. Somehow, I thought the more people I told, that I gave this news to, the less awful it would feel for me. Spread it thin. This turned out to be a terrible plan. Every person I spoke to had questions I couldn't answer. I was drinking steadily as I worked my way through the phone book and ticked off names. I rang the same people twice or three times. I just kept dialling, telling people, "I've got really bad news.

Some said, yes, you just told me five minutes ago.

Paul's parents and sister came over. I felt at home with grief, kidding myself that I was at the centre of it, even, as in all of my bereavements, I was not. My children stared, quiet, bewildered, as people came and went. I poured everyone drinks so I didn't have to get drunk alone. Invariably, they'd stop drinking after one or two, if they drank at all. I didn't stop. I was drinking around the clock now.

The funeral was big, and a big blur. I was so catatonic that I had to go into the spacious disabled toilet to lie down on the cool tiles. When I got up, instead of pulling the lavatory chain, I pulled the emergency one. When I emerged, staggering, from the disabled loo, I saw some people looking concerned. What was the emergency? Everything, and nothing. I thought, I've made a mistake. I am at some random funeral. Paul is in London Fields, walking the dogs.

Paul, I thought, if you weren't dead, I could kill you. I was raging. How dare you leave? Another fucking memory I could not put my arms around. Another reason to remain paralytic for the foreseeable future. I was the queen of self-pity, of the justification to get hammered all the time. I had no template for life after this kind of grief, none that appealed. In the absence of a code of conduct, of dignity, of grace and acceptance, I retreated to the false safety net of online pharmacies and my home bar.

His wife moved in with us, at my insistence. The plan was she would live with us until she figured out a better plan. She was quiet, dignified, enormously sad, but despite her tremendous pain, she was at all times gracious, helpful with the children, and did most of her crying in private. None of us had any ideas for a better plan. The paralysis of grief, and my getting paralytic, made the three of us, at least in the short term, incapable of making any decisions.

Sometime during all this, my husband and I were invited to the 50th birthday party of a childhood friend in Liverpool. I have very little memory of the trip up there or of the party, except that I fell asleep, drunk, in a corner, having pre-loaded at the hotel on the night. The next morning, I knew he was angry and disgusted but we had another engagement, with my uncle and aunt in Chester, and I said, "Can we just have a row amnesty until the lunch is over?"

I remember walking around Chester, my head and stomach throbbing, trying to make conversation that had nothing to do with me getting so rip-roaring drunk the night before. I said, "Wow, look at all the Tudor buildings. Look, there's a town crier. Look, there's the River Dee. Look, you can go up all these little staircases and be on an entire other level of touristy shops." My husband did not respond. In a moment of clarity I really did feel sorry for him. He had not signed up for this.

My aunt laid on a thankfully Spartan lunch, a help-yourself affair of dishes that were very easy on the stomach. We made small talk. At one point my uncle called my husband into his study for a chat. Then my husband came out and asked me to go out into the garden with him. He told me that my uncle had told him that my mother had cancer and I had to go back to the States to be with her. Just more bad news in the shitstorm. I was numb, dumb and dreading the trip over. I pictured myself crying and smoking in the airless, memory-choked flat, while she smiled bravely through it.

Cleaning, Barbican 2014
THE DEAD CONCERT PIANIST

I LIKE THE BARBICAN IN theory but I find its Brutalist mazes and walkways so confusing that I have to factor in at least an hour of getting-lost time before arriving at any job there. "You go under the tunnel," the guy barks down the phone, but before I can say, "Which tunnel?", I am in a tunnel and emerge to find a block of flats that is not his block of flats.

"Which tunnel did you go through?"

"I guess the wrong one, and I was going to call you back but I couldn't get reception because..."

"You were in the tunnel," he finishes for me.

When I finally get to the flat, a split-level, two-bedroom place with a beautiful, dizzying gappy staircase, the kind where you can see the floor beneath you as you go up it, he is in a hurry to leave. My lateness has made him late. He tells me the story quickly.

"This is my father's flat. He's been away. I had... a procedure... so I've been staying here, recuperating, and now he's coming back and well, it needs a deep clean," he says. "But please don't touch the piano. A light dusting, maybe, but don't use any products."

He leaves without any further instruction. I can see this flat is a magnificent museum to someone who has died, I am guessing his mother, by the likeness in the many photographs of her.

There are concert programmes with her face on them, and shelves of musical scores. A dead concert pianist.

There is a small balcony outside, absolutely covered with cigarette butts. I imagine the guy, in his bathrobe, staggering outside for a smoke. In the bedroom, where I assume he has been camping out, recuperating, there is a collection of dusty stuffed-animal toys on the bed. They are too old to be "get well soon" teddies, though there is a deflated metallic "Get well" balloon collapsed by the far end of the bed. This depresses the hell out of me, the deflated message. All around the bed is stuff of illness: balled-up used tissues, empty prescription packets, a basin, a jug, a torn-off hospital ID tag, an empty tin of a nutrition drink. But then, a pristine dressing table with old atomisers, a "vanity set" comprising a heavy silver brush, a mirror and compact on a crystal platter. Bottles of scents that have been discontinued. Scent is one of those things I know about. I know what you can't get any more. They also have a novelty bird clock, which makes the sound of, say, a greater spotted woodpecker, at four o'clock. Except this clock is slightly wrong. At eleven, robin o'clock, it makes the sound of the barn owl, which is six o'clock bird time.

As I clean the flat, and it is a big job, I can feel the grief there. All of her things, untouched. I know these shrines. You feel the dead's presence, in their absence.

The piano is a magnificent grand. The lid is off, the top propped up by one of those sticks, exposing the innards.

He rings me halfway through the clean, to remind me to get rid of any evidence of smoking. So I sweep the balcony spotless, and pour buckets of soapy water over it, mopping away the ashes. When I go back in to make the bed with fresh sheets, I am in two minds as to whether to restore the toys back to the pillows, or put them in a bag, for washing. They creep me out; the eyes are either too big or they are missing, which is worse. I stuff them all in a bag and put them in the cabinet directly above the bed. I have to cram them in; whoever opens it will be hit by a cascade of old, eyeless, dusty animal toys. Why do dusty old toys always feature in horror films about serial killers? What was his "procedure" anyway? A change of identity?

A few hours later, I am at another job, and I get a frantic text: "WHERE ARE THE STUFFED ANIMALS? THEY BELONG ON THE BED!!!"

I feel like saying, "Fuck the stuffed animals. The bird clock is on the wrong bird. This is catastrophic."

I text back: "In the cabinet over the bed, but be careful when you open it."

"FOUND THEM. PEW!"

"Phew!" I text back, cementing our joint relief regarding the restoration of the toys, as well as correcting his spelling. I imagine them falling out over his head, then him gathering them up and putting them in the correct order, the biggest in the middle, the smaller ones at the sides, all of them thickly crusted with dust, holding silent court on the crisp, clean sheets.

Chapter Twenty-One

On the plane to New York. I sit next to a very effusive gay guy who keeps ordering us drinks. I arrive very drunk and stay that way for the whole six-week visit. My mother's cancer is on her spine and she has great difficulty moving. I have to help her get in and out of bed and haul her in and out of taxis, as we go from doctor to hospital, and hospital to another doctor. Though both of us are small, she is a dead weight. I find all these manoeuvres graceless, impossible and desperate. I know her dignity is important, but I can't give her that, as I half pull, half push her into the back of a taxi. She is dosed up on steroids and painkillers, and I think, I can just stay out of it the whole time, she will never know. Drinking and caring go well together, if you get the balance right. You are both on the same sedated page.

It only becomes problematic if there is an emergency. We have to take her to the emergency room at Jamaica Hospital one night. It is attached to a wing called the Trump Pavilion – this is before any of us know this is probably a bad omen. It's like an army field hospital: no divisions between patients, cops handcuffed to gunshot victims on gurneys. Doctors rushing around from patient to patient, speaking that weird medical slang. My mother, in great pain, lies on a gurney five hours, six hours, seven hours. I finally catch one of the running nurses. "Not now," she says, but I jog after her, "My mother, she's in pain..."

And here she stops and looks at me as if I am clinically insane. She sweeps her arm in an introductory gesture, as if to say, "And here we have the emergency room, where every single person is in pain..." I say, "Maybe we could find her doctor? His name is Dr Singh?" Roll of eyeballs. "We have eleven, no, twelve... twelve Dr Singhs. Which one do you mean?"

"The one who is my mother's doctor..."

"I don't have time for this. She'll get seen when it's her turn to get seen..." and she runs off.

Eventually they take her in for surgery and afterwards, she is moved to a convalescent home.

She hates it, hates the place, the food, all the old and sick people. I go to visit her one day and there's an Elvis impersonator on the recreation ward. I say to my mother, "Let's go see fake Elvis," but she doesn't even really like the real one, so I go by myself, leaving my mother with her uneaten tray of awful food, and I sit in an empty wheelchair, watching the fake Elvis murder "Love Me Tender" before a group of old and demented people, literally a captive audience, most of them on the nod on sedatives. One woman throws up all over the floor as the guy sings "Teddy Bear". I have finished the contents of my hip flask and swallowed three or four Valiums and I fall asleep in the wheelchair as Elvis puts on a Stetson and starts singing country songs. Sometime later I am woken by a nurse.

I have no idea where I am or how I got there.

We go to doctors and lawyers and accountants and emergency rooms. When I say go, I mean, stumble, stagger, trip into, fall into. My mum is appointed carers from agencies, some nicer than others. One nicks the one valuable thing she has, a Burberry coat. She catastrophises. "I hate carers; they steal your Burberrys" – as if she has had many carers, or many Burberrys. She's inconsolable about the theft. Almost more so than about the cancer itself. It is just easier to be pissed off about this crime than it is to be pissed off about something she has little control over.

After six weeks, I leave. My sister is at the kitchen table staring at all the bewildering piles of bills and bank statements I've left for her to deal with and she's not OK with me leaving. I've put Post-it notes on top of each pile. The notes are bossy and full of words like "Urgent" or "Do this first!" My mother tells me later that I left my empties all over the flat. I was too pissed or hungover to throw them out or hide the evidence. Empties and demanding Post-it notes. This is the way I communicate with my shrinking world.

Cleaning, Shoreditch 2015
DON'T SAY IT, POST IT

SHE DOES SOMETHING IN FASHION and shares a flat with two other girls. I think they all work crazy hours. She is all angle lines, tidy, unflappable, and I just know I am not going to match her levels of precision. There will be a streak on the glass table, and she will glare at it. The clogged-up conditioner slot of the washing machine, if not entirely de-clogged of conditioner, will irk her. I clean one of the two bathrooms, using every de-streaking trick I have ever studied on those cleaning-hack channels on YouTube. I use an old toothbrush (which I got from Poundland, the cleaner's Nirvana of products) to scrub the grit from the bathtub tiles. The bathroom glistens. This is going to be good. But then one of the girls comes home, unexpectedly, and shuts herself away in the bathroom.

Oh God, please don't be sick. Don't mess up the loo. Don't take a bath. Don't even use the sink, which I have dried with heavy-duty paper towels. Don't touch the taps, which I have scrubbed with limescale remover. In fact, just don't do anything at all, just marvel at how clean it is, how the new loo roll has a bit folded over on a diagonal, like they do in hotels.

Later I get a flurry of unfinished texts. I don't have a smartphone so if anyone tries to send me a picture, I won't get it. She writes words, from China, where she is, and tries to send me photos taken by one of her flatmates who has put Post-it notes on all the bits I did not clean properly, with arrows pointing to the offending mess. When I explain that I can't receive the photos, she texts out their contents. Splattered toothpaste on the mirror. Dustballs under the kitchen table. The garden door left unlocked. A litany of house-cleaning sins, all recorded in Post-it notes.

Insanely, I text her back, in China, terrified about how much it is going to cost me. I write that I did do the bathroom mirror, but her flatmate, uh, must have brushed her teeth right after. Then in caps I write: I APPRECIATE YOUR PRECISION BUT FUCK THIS SHIT. I don't send it. It's too expensive to text China. I just quit the normal way.

Chapter Twenty-Two

I leave my husband and children and Paul's wife, her dogs and my cats, in December 2010. Too many days I am waking up on the floor, unsure how I got there. It is not even that I am developing a tolerance for drink and drugs, rather, a tolerance for the catastrophes that follow a use-up, a binge. I am just too "What evs..." about everything. Sometimes I see I've been sick, with no memory of having been sick. I can't even remember my old phobia of being sick. But when you're that pissed, you can't remember anything. Sometimes I feel I am hovering over my own body, halfway between the floor and ceiling. The only normal thing I do is walk the dogs. I pretend Paul is with me, his gait hurried, frantic, as it was in life. He has told me outrageous lies about the dogs. They don't like cops, he said. They are funny around black people. It's all lies. They just run around, happy to be out, scrambling for discarded chicken bones which I have to prise from their slobbery mouths. Paul can't walk the dogs today. That's what I said to his mother.

I like to walk the dogs on the common at twilight. One night there is a slow drizzle, a dense fog. It reminds me of one time when Paul and I were walking the dogs on Hackney Marshes in the pouring rain, the kind that hits you horizontally. I told Paul, "I'm not having fun any more." And he said yes, it was not fun any more and we would walk very fast, to my flat. We tried to dry the dogs and ourselves off, and I huddled by the kitchen radiator, waiting for the kettle to boil. I felt cosy and calm. Paul leafed through a newspaper. I kept dragging this image up whenever I missed him, which was most of the time.

I must have, at some point, started talking to myself. On the common, in this drizzle, a man comes up to me, very close, and says, "Who are you talking to?" He smells nice, of a particular sandalwood soap I used to buy in health food shops.

I say, "I'm talking to Paul."

He says, "Your dogs, one is called Paul?"

"No, Paul…"

They say if you are properly going mad, you don't know you are going mad. I think at this stage I know I am… not well. Not well in the head. I can't find the words to tell the guy who Paul is. I just want him to stand closer so I can smell the sandalwood soap off his body.

"Why you are crying, pretty lady?"

I hadn't even known I was crying. In those early days, I only noticed when I stopped crying.

"Your man not treating you nice?"

I tell him everything is fine. My man is very nice. I am just sad.

He moves in closer. The dogs, with no protective instinct whatsoever, are far away, hiding in the hedge by the railway line. The man is within kissing distance of my face. He is close enough to smell my breath.

"You drinking. Woman should not drink. Make you sadder." And then he clasps me around the middle, as if he were going to waltz with me. He clasps me around the middle and whispers in my ear, "I like you. I sorry for you. Go back to your man. Stop the sad. Stop the drink." And he gives me a little squeeze and runs off. I run in the direction of the hedge and get the dogs back on their leads. As I walk back to the flat, I know the best thing I can do for my family, possibly for myself, is to leave them. I cannot stop the sad, but I can stop adding to it, magnifying it, appropriating it greedily, all for myself.

This year, 2010, is possibly one of the last years when there is still such a thing as a bedsit in London. I go into the newsagent where I buy the mints to disguise (badly) the alcohol on my breath and see a sign in the window for a room, 60 pounds a week. A badly written note on an index card. I ring the number, and the cheery fellow on the end of the line says I can see the room right then. It is on a side road off the high street of my neighbourhood. The room is situated above a former butcher's shop, which has been converted, barely, into bedsitting rooms. The man who lives downstairs was the original butcher, and is now old, ill, immobile. The room that is to become my home for nearly a year is lined with Indian restaurant-style flock wallpaper, falling off in places, with damp. A big bed, which sags heavily in the middle, takes up most of the room. I punch it, and a billow of dust escapes. I do not yet know I am going to get scabies, bedbugs and repeated asthma attacks from the damp. A wardrobe, a small sink, a small fridge. Bars on the windows. It is freezing. When we speak, curls of breath smoke come out of our mouths. He says he will try to rig up an electric heater. What is unspoken is that the room is uninhabitable. The damp sinks into my bones.

"No wifi," says my soon-to-be landlord, the affable Dennis.

"No problem. I'll take it."

I have no recall of the conversation about my moving out. It is something along the lines of having to sort myself out, it will only be a few months, I will figure something out, there is no one else involved, I am tired of shouting at my daughter, she is tired of being shouted at, I am tired of all the stuff involved with being a mum. All I know is that it is less about running away from my husband, my children, and more about running away from responsibility. I am giving up any pretence of looking after them. I can't even look after myself. The official line I tell myself, and no one else, is that I am planning to lock myself into a Trainspotting-style detox. The real story is, left to my own devices, I will just drink as much as is humanly possible and get my drugs from the men and women who sell them outside the Drug and Alcohol Misuse Team offices in my borough. The best place to buy prescription sedatives is off heroin addicts who sell them to buy heroin. The sedatives are to help them ease off the harder drugs. It's win-win in some respects, except we're all a bunch of losers. To think only a few years ago my biggest buying dilemma was the buy-one, get-one-free offer on baked beans at Morrisons. I used to love doing the weekly shop. The shop music system playing 90s chart music, the looks of sympathy exchanged by mums whose kids are having meltdowns in the trolley seat. I want to tell the guy with the meth-wasted face, the weeping sores on his arms, as I hand him 30 quid and he hands me his blue pills, that this is not really me. I'm the lady singing to my son, who's munching on raisins in the shopping trolley. "I've been driving in my car... it's not quite a Jaguaaaar" – yeah, right, like he's gonna care. We leave these silent transactions in a hurry, wordlessly. I don't count the pills in front of him. Bad form.

I move into the bedsit and start shaking. I am not detoxing. It's just so cold. I stick up some pictures of my kids on the wall with BluTack. Within minutes they fall down, bringing strips of the damp wallpaper with them. Below me on my small strip of road, there is a Caribbean social club and a corner shop that sells alcohol and a variety of foods whose instructions are to become my three favourite words in cookery at that time: just add water. Smash, Pot Noodle, Cup-a-Soup.

My days have a routine. Wake up, feel shaky and sick, go down to the corner shop to buy milk and a tabloid so the guy behind the counter thinks I am a normal person, reading the paper and drinking tea. But I also buy two airplane-size bottles of vodka to stop the shakes and nausea and I always say it like it's an afterthought: "Milk, paper... oh look, your cornflakes are on sale, oh yes, and two of those, down by the cigarettes, no left a bit, no right a bit." It only takes a few visits before I give up the pretence of milk and paper and he just plonks the miniatures down on the counter and I give him the money, and drink the drinks before I even get back up to my room, which is a one-minute walk away, 30 seconds if I run. When you live to drink and drink to live, none of this feels abnormal.

I am stopped in the street by a young, beautiful black woman who says, "I can HELP you, HE can help you", and I think she's got a dealer husband or something, but actually, she is married to a pastor. She says, "Come to our church on Sunday," and she takes my number to ring me to remind me to come, and I'm like yeah, whatever, I'll come.

I go to the church at the appointed time, held in the same community hall where my kids used to take art lessons from a French lady. The preacher looks quite like Martin Luther King Jr, my childhood hero, and I think he's going to say he has a dream, because I am pissed and reality and fantasy are blurred. The preacher and his wife greet me as "sister", and everybody is sister or brother or son or daughter and I think they are all related, except me, but they are going to adopt me so that's OK. I can be the white drug addict sister they save.

Martin Luther King Jr gives a PowerPoint presentation, and during the hymns, which are all Gospel, which I kind of like, the words come up on the screen – it's like God karaoke – and I am singing and clapping and feeling kinda spiritual, kinda black, still as pissed as I can possibly be without falling down, but feeling some communal, PowerPoint-presentation love.

When I am not at church, or drinking or sleeping, I go to the Somalian internet caff. I send emails to people

I barely knew a long time ago, in Boston, in New York. I write about a life which is funnier and more interesting than my own. I put on grubby headphones, with the foam poking out, and watch bits of episodes of TV programmes I watched as a child, or I watch old videos of the Jackson Five. Every half-hour I take a swallow from a water bottle full of vodka.

Sometimes Mustapha, who runs the internet shop, is the only human I talk to all day. After he finds out that I am by birth American, he starts calling me Michelle Obama and we laugh riotously at the joke, as if every time is the first time he is making it or I am hearing it. "Booth seven, Michelle Obama. First you watch your pop music Michael Jackson, alriiightt, faaaar out, then is education time. I show you film about what is happening in Somalia. It very sad."

So it starts. In booth seven, I am jiggling about in my seat to "ABC", watching the five loon-trousered brothers dance and sing, and then I drink and write long letters to people I hardly know. Maybe we worked together in a bar for a month, 30 years ago. It's a connection. Then I join Mustapha at the crumbling counter and he turns his screen so I can see the film about Somalia, and he translates the voiceover for me.

"She is walking across the desert to find water. Her baby is dead and she has to bury it. Her other children are dead. Soon she will die as well." I burst into tears and stuff money in the jar. I have money vaguely earmarked for things like food, or laundry, or electricity, but it all goes on drinks and drugs or internet or the Somalian refugees.

One day Mustapha looks distressed. He explains that his wife, who has just had another baby, is alone and lonely and sad. After the shop closes, will I go with him to Tottenham to offer company and solace to his wife?

I don't think I'm really good company. But when he pulls the shutters down, I climb into his car and he drives us to Tottenham. We arrive at a shabby flat and there is a woman in the kitchen, a baby in a sling on her front, and a toddler in a sort of playpen/cage in the front room, watching a video, the same video, of the starving woman in Somalia. I try to change the channel to *Teletubbies*.

The woman speaks no English and I speak no Somalian. I want to express so many things to her, that my relationship with her husband is that of customer and internet shop guy, that I have two children myself, and that in less isolation, in less dire circumstances, I walked out on them. That I know how sore her breasts are (and I try to mime this, to much hilarity from her – post-birth tits, the international mime language), that I know how long the days are, that I know what it is like to go for days on end without speaking to anyone. It is impossible to express such complex things in sign language. Instead, I hold the baby and she goes back into the kitchen to cook up some stew. The baby has a long, beautiful Somalian neck and is peaceful in my arms.

Mustapha talks to his wife and says to me that she wants me to come back. She will make a meal. But my stomach lurches at the thought of food. I invent a sudden job. I tell him I have a job in a... care home. Night shifts. He nods gravely. "English people, they don't look after their families." Wow, he's seen right through me. I am not looking after mine. He gives me a lift back to my bedsit. Before I get out of the car, I tell him I think it is important for his wife to meet people who speak her language. He looks desperate and upset, and says, "But you will come back, yes? She needs you! Women need women."

I lie, "I'll try."

Cleaning, London 2015
I DID PHONE SEX IN YOUR LOFT

THERE ARE SOME JOBS YOU walk into the first day and know you are never coming back. For one day, back in the early 90s, I was a phone-sex operator. We all sat round in a U-shaped desk formation, trying to keep guys on the phone by talking dirty. Minimum wage, the fast-food joint of sex. It was in East London and the shift was all night. I was terrible at it. A guy on the phone asked what I was wearing and I said, "Um, jeans and like one of those lumberjack sort of shirts," and he slammed the phone down. The girl next to me was mainlining a family-sized bucket of KFC and faking orgasms every five minutes – clinically obese, dermatologically challenged, but BRILLIANT at talking dirty. I came off shift at 7am, bleary-eyed, feeling dirty, having failed to talk dirty all night, knowing I would not be returning to this job.

Over 20 years later, I find myself in the very same road I did the bad phone sex in, another lifetime ago. A lot of the wholesale trade garment shops are still there but many of the warehouses have been converted into giant living spaces with exposed bricks and beams and very special flooring that needs to be cleaned with mail-order products. I knock on the brass knocker with a feeling of déjà vu and dread. I'm lost in a reverie of telling some guy, on his mobile phone on his tractor in the middle of a field so his wife wouldn't catch him, that I was wearing lacy underwear and feeling "hot for you" in a voice so robotic it made Stephen Hawking sound like Mariella Frostrup, when the door opens and reveals an extremely slim woman with a tiny pregnancy bump. The place is gleaming, shimmering, as if she has been cleaning all night or has had another cleaner in. The ground floor is immaculate; white tiled, shiny, industrial, like a fancy office floor that has just been industrially cleaned and waxed. The kitchen island bears a big carved wooden bowl of fruit, and is lined with top-of-the-range oils and wines and spices. I am about to break the ice, to say, "You know, last time I was here, I was trying to be dirty, and how ironic that now I am here to clean," but I can tell she is on a tight schedule. Not one for small talk. She shows me the cupboard under the rush-matting stairs. She shows me how each cleaning product is clearly labelled to designate which room, which surface, and should I mix anything up, it will really damage the surface, so really, please, read the labels carefully.

We had spoken on the phone beforehand. She said her other cleaner had left or was sick and the place was an absolute tip, she couldn't stand it, etc. Could this be the place she was talking about? I run a finger over a bookshelf. Dustless and gleaming. Every surface is spotless. and as clean as clean can be. Every pillow plumped, every tap as shiny as a new mirror. Three floors of this impossible-to-replicate perfection. I can tell it is going to look worse after I've wiped all the clean things down one more time, fighting off invisible germs, invisible dirt, for this extremely neatly pregnant woman with her tiny, tidy bump. I go over each surface, as advised, with each special product. This one smells of lemons, the special bathroom tile stuff smells strong and makes my eyes sting, the wood polish smells like the Body Shop at Christmas, sort of woodsy and over-powering.

In the main bedroom, there are expensive high heels in a certain order. That's an easy one. You move them about in a different order so they know you've hoovered.

Underneath the bed, there are more shoes in boxes, and an old-fashioned mask, red, cat's-eye shaped, and some furry handcuffs. Leftover hen do clobber, or part of their sexual routine? This stuff you don't move, because you don't want them to know you've seen it. On her side, a stack of books about pregnancy and what to expect. On his side, travel guides and cufflinks.

When the clean is done, the house looks markedly worse, as I knew it would. She texts me and says she doesn't think I am a "good fit" but thanks me for my effort. We meet a few days later, in the rain, outside the Tube station. I hand her the keys and say good luck with the baby. She thanks me, curtly. I wonder what products she will use to clean her poor kid when it pops out.

Chapter Twenty-Three

These bedsit years lack the romance and flighty devil-may-careism of the bedsit years in my 20s. No wacky neighbours writing bad poetry and trying to get me to fix their novels or love lives. This is just me, alone, sleeping, drinking, doing drugs, waiting for the elusive British weather to emerge, the sort where you can't see the wisps of exhaled air outside the multitude of coats and blankets that cover your shivering body. Off-licence, drink, drugs, nap, internet shop, drink, drugs, crying over Somalian internet newsfeed. No one tells you how small and boring life becomes, when life is no longer becoming. How quickly a feeling of freedom turns into loneliness.

I make a minor attempt to change my routine by attending a local yoga class, some sort of free trial. It is full of new mums trying to get their figures back, and people with made-up, hard-to-pronounce spiritual names they adopted after doing an intensive yoga course some-where in India. Of course I am half-cut, as always, and worry that the whole concept of balancing on one leg to be "a tree" will result in bona fide injury or total collapse.

There is a lot of emphasis on breathing correctly. I know if I exhale in the noisy, show-offy way the oth-ers do, I will totally stink out the room with my fetid, vodka breath. But people are farting all over the shop and women are asking questions like, "I have my period. Is it OK to do an inverted posture?" It seems a safe place to have bad breath and collapse. They have these rubber band things to increase resistance. I suppress a great desire to ping my one, playfully, at the farting woman in front of me. One pose, with arms stretched sideways, reminds me of the poses in "Walk Like an Egyptian". I start to do the whistling bit of the song. The teacher comes up to me and puts a finger over her mouth. I say, "I am trying to breathe correctly, but I can only do this by whistling 'Walk Like an Egyptian'."

"You are intoxicated," she hisses.

"Distinct possibility."

"I think you need to leave the class."

So I do, walking like an Egyptian. I think I am hilarious but I am not oblivious to the whispers and stares of the women, who are now standing like warriors in lycra. I leave before they charge at me. The yoga warriors are ferociously calm, aggressively Zen. If, in my dream of dreams, I could ever be calm without drugs, I would prefer a more sedate form of calm.

A few days later, in another half-hearted attempt to change things, I sign up for a borough-sponsored, reduced-drinking programme. I am counting units of drink, writing them down in a diary and then subtracting five or six units because I don't want them to know how much I am drinking. Everybody does this. And everybody knows, particularly the counsellors, that, whatever we write down, there's more that we are not writing down. This is not the cutesy world of "Five units, V. Bad" Bridget Jones, but the insane world of Bottle of Jack, not enough, get more. A few days a week, a group of us meet in a basement off London Fields and we talk about how we feel before we drink. We are an emotionally stunted group. We've forgotten, collectively, what it feels like before we have the first one. It's too automatic. The facilitator says, "What are you feeling before you pick up, Michele?" I say, "I feel like having a drink", and the other drunks nod knowingly. For one session a week, they get in an auricular acupuncturist, who sticks needles in our ears to reduce the craving for drink. We sit in a circle, with needles in our ears, sweating that funky drink sweat people do when their livers pack up. "Don't answer your mobile," I say to the guy next to me. "You'll perforate your eardrum."

After the guy takes the needles out, I go down to the pub with two friends I've made in the group. Our ears feel sore. Our clothes are falling off us. We pass the playground in London Fields and I see mothers hovering over their shrieking children, pushing them on swings, going down the slide with them, kissing scraped knees, offering raisins out of little plastic tubs.

I say to my friends, "Let's stop for a minute. I want to watch the children play."

"Nah, they'll think we're perverts."

"We're not perverts, we're just drunks."

So we stop and I watch this scene; something is coming back to me. I say, "No, you don't get it, I used to do this."

My friend says, "So what? We were all kids, once."

"No, I was a mum. I think I still am. I dunno."

I do not cut down my drinking on the reduced-drinking programme. I just tell more lies and occasionally drink with friends instead of alone.

My friend introduces me to the Drug and Alcohol Misuse Team at my local council, which can sponsor people to do a residential rehab. I have to go to interviews to show that I am determined, that I really want this. I don't really want it. It's the last thing I want. But I have to pretend I really want this. I can see that my skin is turning yellow. I need injections of vitamins because I am not eating. Food takes up valuable stomach space reserved for alcohol.

I sit in an office in Hackney council's services building and stare at my feet. A woman with an air of "Here comes another one…" sits across from me and says, "I can never tell who will be OK and who will go back out into the madness. I'm not sure about you. What do you think? You think you can do this? Do you really want this?"

"I think I can't keep doing what I am doing. But I'm scared to not do it."

She writes some things down on a sheet of paper and tells me the next step of the process. It's sort of like a kindergarten for rehab. Daily classes in a local centre, to teach you what rehab will be like.

In one of the first lessons, a guy comes in to tell us about his experience of rehab. He looks like Huggy Bear from *Starsky and Hutch*, with that jive ass walk and hand thing going on. He tells us rehab is not for pussies. I get up to leave the room.

"Where are you going," asks the facilitator.

"I am a pussy," I wimper.

"Get yo pussy ass back in here," says Huggy. I don't really have a choice.

He uses all this drug and street slang, talking about the problems of coming back "into your area", your "manor", and your old contacts trying to get you to score. He says the first few weeks you are pretty sick, then you go to all these meetings and people just tell you all their shit all day and then guys in the street – there are dealers everywhere – spot the ones in rehab and try to lure them back.

Oh God. How did it come to this, talking about manors and dealers? I should be picking up my kids from school, monitoring "screen time" and making ice lollies out of 100 per cent fruit juice. I have the knowledge to be a good mum, I just feel constitutionally incapable of sticking to the script.

He says rehab works. He is now employed as a chef. "I don't chop lines any more. Just heritage carrots." He terrifies me, his story terrifies me. What the fuck is a heritage carrot? I think rehab will kill me or turn me into a chef. Still, I go back to the office of the first woman, who says she will present my case before a panel, and they will decide if I am worthy of a council-sponsored rehabilitation programme.

She gives me some brochures on the centres the council endorses. I look mainly at the ones by the seaside. These tend to be situated in the less salubrious part of town. I like the crumbling bits of the seaside, the faded grandeur, the peeling paint, the abandoned chippies and rock shops, the dirty beaches. I know this bit of England. Towns with high levels of unemployment, obesity, mobility scooters and charity shops. Oh, they didn't say all this in the brochures. They are all about compassion and success rates and glowing men and women doing something un-junkily sporty, like flying a kite on a beach. I choose Bournemouth, where I went on a family holiday some years ago.

I remember thinking this was not the Martin Parr English seaside of lobster-coloured obese people shouting at their children to come in from the water because the ice creams were here. This was a strange seaside full of thin Goths: pale, spotty, jerking, looking as if sunlight would kill them, walking slowly, haltingly, sitting in the little wind-shelter enclaves looking out to sea. Now I was going to join the ranks of these transparent ghost people, and how different it would look to me now. A few years ago, the seaside had been a jolly outing. I'd be supervising my children, floating in rubber tubes in the shallows of the sea. I'd be reapplying sunscreen to wriggling bodies. Buying a new ice cream after one fell on the boardwalk. Buying a new balloon for the one that floated away. We'd get back to the sandy, damp-smelling holiday flat and stick the little brown bodies in the bath. Then I would go out again to wander through the icy-cold displays at the Co-op, looking for vegetarian nuggets in the shape of fast food.

Now I was devoid of all that responsibility. I would be able to wander, invisible, except to others in rehab. The woman organising my rehab rings me the night before they secure the funding. "You are going tomorrow morning. Pack your bag."

Of course, I get good and proper loaded the night before, packing willy-nilly, throwing a nightgown, some jumpers, underwear and, inexplicably, a hammer and nails into my case. My bedsit's dimensions are such that the suitcase takes up all the floor space. I pass out drunk and fall out of bed onto the hard edge of the suitcase, and find myself unable to breathe. I call my friend Khanyi who comes over. I can't move or breathe, so she calls an ambulance. The paramedic tells me I've broken two ribs, possibly more but if I go to hospital they won't be able to do anything. I thank them for the information and apologise for wasting their time. When they leave, I crawl into the suitcase, which is easier to get to than the bed, and try to figure out a way to breathe that doesn't hurt.

By the morning the pain is extreme. Khanyi comes and takes me and my case down to Paddington. She helps me carry the case onto the train.

"What have you got in here?" she asks. "Carpentry tools?"

"Yeah."

Apart from breathing, I almost enjoy the trip down, that bit where London is not London any more, and you see animals, and fields, and you get all excited, as if it is the first time you have seen such things. I have a bottle of vodka to finish before we hit Bournemouth.

When I get to the place, most of the clients are away on a field trip. I sit in a large room, half watching a film about a tsumani, all that water rushing up out of nowhere

– my first rehab guilt trip: you have done this to yourself! Those people didn't chose to be swept away by a giant wave.

Eventually I am interviewed by a man so smiley and glossy-eyed, I find it unnerving. Then I am escorted to a GP who looks at my ribs, tells me what I knew and what he is not allowed to give me during detox (proper painkillers) and asks me to dump all my drugs on the table. I am desperately sad, giving all my drugs away. I am already thinking of where I can find more.

By half four I am escorted to my lodgings, a house shared with other people whose rehab has mostly been sponsored by the council. My room – monk-like, a bed, a wardrobe and sink – smells like unwashed feet.

We go, as a house, to some fellowship meeting that night, people using language and chants and sayings I do not understand. I just follow the pretty girl with the long red hair. She is my unofficial minder, my recovery buddy.

The meeting is full of all these guys who look like bikers who did a lot of drugs in the 60s, "when drugs were really drugs". They use slang I do not understand, they talk about standing on top of a car park, one guy going on about a bag of brown going into his pound coin. Pound coin: groin, brown: heroin. My minder translates for me.

That first night of detox, I have strange, sweaty dreams about dead people swimming in the cold and stony sea. I wake up in a cold sweat, then hot, then cold. It will be like this for the next six weeks.

Two of the other women in the house are mothers, so

we all call each other "Mum". The house seems divided into little groups, even though there are only six of us. I just stay glued to the pretty red-haired woman, my chain-smoking minder. Sometimes I knock on the door of one of the mums. Her room is vast. On her desk, she has a school photo of one of her girls, the classic missing-a-front-tooth photo, with the summer uniform of red-and-white check and a high pony tail. The pony tail is a sporting girl's hair arrangement.

I say, "Mum, your gal does sport?"

"Yes, Mum. Gymnastics, dance, street dance, football. I used to do all those myself..."

I can see her face, now haggard but still retaining some youth, in her daughter's cheeky smile.

"You got pictures of your two?"

"No, I didn't want to bring them. I don't need reminding of... what I left."

We are having an Indian summer in September, the weather warm enough to hit the beach. The people in my house watch music videos blasted at full volume all the time. Ed Sheeran's "The A Team" is in the charts, a song about a girl selling her body to get Class As. Everything is strange and new and sad to me. I know there must be something terribly wrong with me if I cry watching MTV. Watching Ed Sheeran.

Then my body comes up in angry, itchy welts. The "foot" smell is a sign of a massive bedbug invasion. We have to leave the flat to have it fumigated, and decamp to a B and B for a few days.

Emaciated, covered in sores, with broken ribs, stumbling

about in a tapered drug-withdrawal haze, punctuated by moments of sheer terror, I am broken. All I know how to do at this point is follow the red-haired girl. Follow the plume of exhaled cigarette smoke. One of the key workers has to find us suitable accommodation and briefs us on how to just sort of pretend to be a group of people on holiday together. Don't tell them we are from rehab, he says. Don't mention the bedbugs.

We file into a flock-wallpapered B and B and go into our rooms. When we come down to the lounge, our host smiles nervously and the least shy of our group barks, "We're on holiday, right!" He smiles as if he's just remembered the answer to the winning question in a pub quiz. We all nod fervently, saying, "Holiday... lovely."

We are all sitting on the floral couch, some of us scratching, jerking, kicking, getting the sweats. A normal group of normal people on a normal seaside break. At breakfast in the morning, I can only half fill my teacup because otherwise I will spill it. The housemates who have already detoxed are always starving, particularly for sweet things, and lots of the pastries go up sleeves, down jumpers and inside hoodies. Then we have to make our way to the centre, where we sit in circles and listen to or tell the most appalling tales.

Every few days they make a small cut in my Valium, exposing some fresh layer of withdrawal and emotional pain. Everything makes me cry. This one guy tells the most horrendous story of addiction and crime and overdoses and prison and death. He is near the end of rehab and doing really well but I am sobbing over his past. He says to me, "Why are YOU crying? This is my shit!" And I sob, "I don't know! Everything makes me cry. Ed fucking Sheeran makes me cry!"

Once again, I am overstepping the concentric circles of misery. The person who is directly affected by the misery has every right to moan. The people in that person's inner circle – the spouse, the kids, the parents – they, too, have a claim to sadness that is over and above the people in the next circle out, who might be close friends. I am stealing this guy's grief, once again stepping into the first circle when I am way out on the outskirts – in this particular case, in a different country, on a different planet.

I see my counsellor and tell him I am really not as bad as all these criminals and Class A drug users. My pathetic protests of "But I never did crime, I never tried suicide, I never stole stuff, I never did sex work, I never did that many illegal drugs," followed by "I'm just your garden variety housewife with a garden variety pill habit" fall on sympathetic but deaf ears. "You stole a mother from your children," he says. I consider this, and tell him, "That's the biggest crock of shit I've ever heard."

Later, back in my small room, I see the truth in his words. I am appalled.

One night, my minder and mentor T and I are straggling behind the others from our flat on our way to a fellowship meeting. Most of these are held in cold church halls, but this one is in a community centre next to another hall, and this lovely, old-fashioned dance music is booming from it. Ballroom dancing. I say to T, let's see what's going on in there. So we climb the steps (this is no easy feat, when detoxing from Valium: your body often spasms, so I have to hold onto her, but she is used to it) and we peer inside. Women in their 50s, 60s, 70s, dancing with men of a similar age, all waltzing perfectly around the room. Everyone dressed up to the nines. Everyone doing the exact same thing, beautifully, gracefully, the women in particular decked out in very flash, sequinned fit-and-flare dresses, with matching high heels. The music is tinny and loud, one-two-three, one-two-three, and they go round and round the room, lost in a reverie of glamour and timing. The hall smells of aftershave and hair-smoothing products. One woman waltzes and wafts past me and I catch a scent of her perfume. My senses are sharpening as the drugs wear off. "She's wearing my scent," I whisper. "We could be friends…" T looks at me doubtfully. Then we stare some more. We are transfixed, enchanted. I grab onto T's sleeve and say, "Let's not go to the meeting. Let's join in the dancing instead. I'm sure we could pick it up." Of course, I have forgotten about my detox-induced spasticity.

"Another time", T says gently, and we dutifully troop into the unsexy, unmusical room in the adjacent building and pick up our cups of instant coffee and take broken Rich Teas off the plate. More tales of woe and redemption. But I am lost in the memory of the ballroom dancers. Next door, there is life, waltzing around the room in painful shoes: this is the very key to everything glorious, not sitting on a hard chair, with cold coffee, listening to someone talk ever so frankly about putting heroin in his testicles after all the other veins had collapsed.

Since that time I have always been instantly attracted to rooms vast enough for dancing to occur. In my mind, as I mop them, I imagine them filled with fragrant ladies and gentlemen with their hair slicked back, dancing, swapping partners with permission, stopping for punch, just the one, as they don't want to mess up their timing or posture.

Cleaning, London 2014
THE CHURCH HALL

THREE MORNINGS A WEEK I clean at a drop-in centre I attended when I got out of rehab. It is adjacent to a beautiful church, with a large community hall. There is a church cat, for catching mice. I can hear the cat before I see him, sometimes padding gracefully over the wooden floor, sometimes meowing, sometimes, with a mouse in his mouth. It's not my job to mop the floor of the community hall, but I like to start my clean by going into the hall, and waltzing by myself.

I go outside for a fag. I can't remember why I started smoking. I guess it's the last acceptably bad thing you can do to your body. Outside the church, there is a ruddy-faced woman sweeping up leaves that fall from the trees. She has no way of getting out of the cold, just sweeping up leaves and crisp packets which will accumulate again within minutes. At least I can get into the warmth of the centre and switch on the radio. They have all these nostalgia stations now so you can transport yourself back to the decade when the clock radio blasted you out of bed before you had a chance to press the snooze button. I tune mine to a 70s station to pretend I am still young, waiting for the Jackson Five to come on.

I get out my mop and my Hoover (called Henry: I like this personification; it makes me feel less alone) and start in the airless toilets, pouring chemicals down the loos, hiding the human smells with something that will some day undoubtedly kill all the fish. Sometimes, in the all-purpose art room, there is a whiteboard covered with a mind map of triggers for using or drinking: loneliness, boredom, hunger, pain, memories. There are posters everywhere for outreach programmes and back-to-work schemes that promise a better life. I have seen posters like this down at the job centre. They're always of a smiling black guy in a chef's hat. Or an Indian girl with a call-centre headset, smiling in front of a computer. I swish my mop around and do a little dance to late-70s Bowie.

During this clean, I have short bursts of happiness. I no longer attend the centre as a client or student, having voluntarily left a couple of years before. I am earning money. Not much, but enough to pay my rent if I work most days.

On Wednesdays I clean the part of the centre where those who are homeless, usually through addiction, drop in for breakfast and a chat. In the offices of the people who run the drop-in, there are boxes and boxes of donations of clothing, toiletries and strange, incongruous food. Jars of lobster bisque. Polish chocolate. Popping candy. The clothes are in boxes which have been used for costumes for an amateur production of *Macbeth*. As I peer into one of the opened boxes, I can see that there are still some Shakespearean costumes – red velvet vests and man tights, and boned bodices. I am trying to imagine the guys at the drop-in centre, layering up with these man tights and vests and bodices. Maybe, for one night only, East London will be awash with men on meths, playing Macbeth. The image of

Shoreditch as one giant Shakespearean drama is enough to kill the tedium of the actual cleaning job. The beauty of a job with minimal human contact is, you can think about anything. The horrible thing about a job with minimal human contact is, you can think about all the humans you used to know, who really want no contact with you.

Chapter Twenty-Four

The standard rehab programme is twelve weeks long, so we have people in our flat graduating – a proper ceremony, with everyone gathered together to say how wonderful you are, a picture of you when you first went in, to compare with a picture of you now, cheeks a bit fuller, make-up on, on a natural rehab high, unaware of the hell that awaits when you get home – and new people coming in.

When one of our house members graduates and leaves, we get Manic Knife Guy – at first, like so many others, boasting about all the big drug deals he's done, all the danger he has been in, how he was into knives, that was his thing, knives. He could cut people up. He would cut people up. He's just about five feet tall, but hard and ravaged by heroin. He arrives at the flat in tattered, knife-shredded clothes, clucking (coming off heroin) but still boasting about what a bad guy he is, all the while chucking up over the balcony during his comedown. I am concerned about the knife thing. What constitutes a knife-wielding error? This I want to know, so as to not commit one.

The first few days he babbles, sometimes in English, sometimes in French. He detoxes with Valium and drops them all over the flat. I give him his Valium back with showbiz exaggeration: "HERE ARE YOUR PILLS WHICH I FOUND ON THE FLOOR AND AM GIV-ING BACK TO YOU BECAUSE THEY ARE YOURS", because I want witnesses and applause to this great act of honesty. That, plus I don't want him to stab me.

After his detox, he emerges as this entirely different person: gentle, soft-spoken, slightly puzzled as to how he got into rehab.

The change in him, in such a small space of time, is seismic. He goes from being a knife-wielding arsehole to a small, sorry man who says very little, except to express regret for the things he's done wrong.

Now we are in October and still enjoying an Indian summer. One day, some of the houses get together and go to the beach. Those who are in better condition start a five-a-side beach football match, with ten or twelve people on each team. They swap sides in the middle of the game, quit, break all the rules, literally move the goalposts. They make up the rules as they go along, laughing, sulking, swearing, finding any excuse to do that goalscoring thing guys do, which is to lift their shirts to cover their heads and run about, blinded by fabric and sweat.

T and I watch from the sides, amused when a small dog joins in the game and scores a goal for one of the teams. The other side is more amused than pissed off when the doggie goal is allowed to stand. I leave T to have a chat with a guy who, like me, was once in media. He's a bit older, a broadcast veteran, and very well-poken and witty. While we are chatting, the woman who owns the dog comes up to us and asks if we are part of the football party. My new friend says, "Yes, we are but, as you can see, we are not playing the game. But, well done, your dog!"

She takes in the scene. The guys covered head to toe with prison tatts, the thin pale girls with scars.

She asks my friend, "So you are a group? But what is it that, um, brings you together?"

"DRINK!" barks my friend.

"Well, drugs as well," I add, for accuracy.

She smiles nervously and calls for her dog. "Walkies!"

One day, a sullen teenager comes to our house. He is eighteen, a chronic weed smoker, and is very angry. As the dulling effects of the Valium wear off, my mood blackens and the teenager becomes the focal point of my bad temper. But what right do I have to tell this spotty, sulking hulk of a thing to wash up after himself, to not play his music so loudly, to wash his clothes now and then, when I have abandoned my own teenage son and daughter, leaving all that adolescent bother to my husband?

About six weeks into my programme, my husband comes down with my son for a visit. I can see my boy is about twelve inches taller than I remember him. I pride myself on my memory, drug addled but seemingly intact in all things spatial. My son takes up more space. Something follicular is going on under his chin and on his upper lip as well. His voice has changed, but it had probably changed when I was living in the bedsit... I just didn't notice. Suddenly this man-child is here, so big, with a deep voice, so different. It feels way worse than for the working mums who miss their child's first steps, because this would have happened over months and I didn't have a clue. I thought... where is my little boy? What happened? Who stole his child's voice and replaced it with this gravelly, quiet and mumbling one? He has just turned fifteen, but he still wants a Halloween costume. We go into town and I get him an orange jump-suit so he can be a Guantanamo Bay inmate. It all feels so normal. He comes out of the dressing-room, a grinning orange thing.

"You look great," I exclaim, "just like a real prisoner."

He looks at me dolefully and says, "You don't have to... try so hard."

"Um, OK, you don't look so great. You look like a juvenile delinquent sent to reform school for stabbing his parents."

"Huh?"

Then we get some junk food, while my husband explores the town. A wave of sadness comes down on me as we sit in KFC, my son with his chips, me with my watery tea. This is what estranged fathers do with their kids at weekends. It's the awkwardness of not knowing how they have changed from one week to the next, how likes are now vehemently disliked, how the band they loved is now "for losers". Last week he liked ketchup, but this week it's mayonnaise. Only it's not a weekly gap for me. I do not really know my children any more, if I knew them that well in the first place.

That evening, I walk my son back to the B and B where

he and my husband are staying. I feel well. I climb onto
my husband's bed and try to snuggle up to him, but he
stiffens, like a child being hugged by an auntie wearing
too much cologne, and I know in that second it is all over.
There is no undoing what I have undone so spectacularly,
so dramatically, so selfishly. I cannot have my husband
and teenagers back. They have made a life without me,
while I was drifting away on my narcotic cloud in the
bedsit. I have traded them in for this strange household of
crack-addicted mums, ex-cons, the stroppy teen, the stabbing guy and a woman who just projectile vomits. I am a
middle-aged version of the stroppy teen I so despise, this
teen I am living with instead of my own rather nice ones.
When I get back to the flat, it's dark. I sit in silence with
T on the balcony and smoke.

One of my friends in rehab comes round in the morning with a CD for me. It is PJ Harvey's *Let England Shake*.
I am shaking for England. England, this little part of it,
politely, is shaking with me.

"What the fucking fuck am I supposed to do? I've lost
everything," I wail. In rehab, all rhetorical questions are
literal ones. I want answers.

He stands by, helplessly. I have seen wives or husbands
picked up from rehab by spouses they had abandoned
– they've come in four-by-fours, two kids, toddlers perhaps, in the back seat, to collect the newly well, rehabili-
tated husband or wife. That is not going to be my story.
I also know I can't go back to drink and drugs. I feel like
I am on a plane circling the airport, in a queue to land.
The land, my life, is right there below me, but just as I

think I am about to hit the runway, the plane tilts, dizzy-
ingly, and starts another circle. I don't know where home
is any more.

Getting Clean, 2011

I AM IN A TWELVE-STEP recovery meeting in Bournemouth. Hard-looking men and women, all of uncertain age. It is very difficult to tell people's ages in recovery. (Heroin, if pure enough, can make you look younger, though I wouldn't recommend it as a youth-enhancing treatment. Crack cocaine is terrible for ageing as it melts any youthful flesh from the face. Benzos, my poison, paradoxically make you worried about where you'll get the next one, which is ageing to the forehead).

Armed robbery to the left of me, GBH to the right, attempted murder to the rear and drug dealer to the front – almost everyone in this meeting has done time in prison.

Me? I have almost been investigated by the DEA. I have nicked pills from my sister and my friend's parents' medicine cabinet. I have gone to a doctor who writes prescriptions in exchange for cash but I have not "done bird".

In terms of hard crime, I feel like Arlo Guthrie in *Alice's Restaurant*, sitting on the group bench with father-rapers, the lone hippie done for littering and creating a nuisance.

Some guy is telling a story about injecting heroin into his balls because he can't find a good vein. Haven't I heard this before? What is it with guys injecting their balls? We eat biscuits and drink tea as he segues into deep-vein thrombosis. If I close my eyes, I could be at a very weird coffee morning.

Chapter Twenty-Five

There is a time, a bit past the eight-week mark, when I start to almost enjoy rehab. It is downright handy living with people who have been to prison for breaking and entering when you forget your keys, for example. In no time, these guys will shimmy up the pipe, slide through an impossibly small window gap and retrieve them for you. I start to enjoy the outings. Bowling is always funny. We are really trying to look normal, but it is impossible. One poor guy, his body covered in morphine patches, is so out of it, he tries to bowl himself down the aisle to knock down the pins. Every few days, he is wearing one or two fewer patches. He's like a badly sewn Guy Fawkes dummy. The more patches they remove, the more he wakes up, and falls apart. He doesn't like being awake, so he leaves.

Another day, for another outing, we go to kickboxing. There is really nothing more visually hilarious then getting a bunch of not so elegantly wasted people together in a gym to try and punch punching pads to the point of passing out, being sick, or both. I am punching this pad this girl is holding and she is as strong as an ox. I know that, when it is my turn to hold the pad for her to punch, I will be horribly injured or dead. She punches a few times, not so hard, then really whacks the pad and I go flying and wind up lying on my back for the rest of the session, thinking, I am at a seaside resort, in winter, and someone is trying to punch my lights out. I'm loving it. It's what I deserve.

It is coming up to Christmas. We fetch an old plastic tree out of the attic and throw some tinsel on it. All the supermarkets have cheap deals on booze. We are meant to avoid the drink aisle completely but it is hard not to stare at the cheap cream sherry and port. Wouldn't one, just one, be so nice, that slight burn at the back of the throat, the warming of the stomach? I stare longingly but am roused out of my reverie by the voice of one of my housemates over the supermarket loudspeaker system. He has grabbed the mic at the front of the shop and he is saying for the whole supermarket to hear, "Will Michele kindly leave the drinks aisle, there is nothing for you there, Miss. Move on."

One night, there is a light snow falling and my friend G and I are lagging behind the others on the way to a fellowship meeting. We stop in front of a brightly lit house, the light from the telly and the Christmas tree flashing in the window. There is a family on the sofa, watching *EastEnders*, passing a box of Quality Street back and forth. I want to go into the house and eat sweets, and watch telly.

I say to G, "Do you think if we knock on the door and act really nice, they will invite us in, for sweets and telly?"

He says he doesn't think so but we both stand, transfixed by the scene. Watching them watching telly.

I say, "Do you think we can ever live like that again, watching telly with our kids, eating sweets, getting ready for Christmas?"

"Dunno. Doubt it."

We walk in silence in the dark and frozen night. To stay well, to stay clean, I will have to spend the rest of my life sitting in cold church halls or community centres, listening to people's stories about being reborn, about rock bottoms, about doing service, about life just getting better and better. Really? A life in which I am never quite warm enough to remove my coat. Shitty coffee, broken biscuits, hard plastic chairs, miserable stories. There is so much to hate about recovery, but it's all I have.

I feel so nervous and uncomfortable and restless at these meetings. A woman I meet in rehab teaches me how to knit so I have something to do with my shaky detoxing hands. I sit in the back, near the door, and knit as some ex-drug dealer talks about his flash car, his narrow escapes, his Rolexes, how many times he was clinically dead, how if he hadn't found "the rooms" (i.e. meetings) he would be in jail or dead, and everyone nods in recognition. I stare blankly and drop stitches.

"Look for the similarities, not the differences," they admonish me, and I say, "This guy was running coke and heroin and eventually living in crack dens. I was a housewife on medically prescribed drugs," and they say, "So are you thinking you are less of an addict than he is, that you are better than him?"

I reply, "Not exactly lesser, but more pathetic. A bit crap. Crap at addiction. But also crap at not being addicted. I'm more your Valley of the Dolls sort of addict."

"Compare and despair," they say.

I like this cutesy bon mot. Who thinks 'em up? Yes, so much of my misery, in addiction and in recovery, and inbetween, is caused by comparing my shoddy life with the seemingly shinier ones around me. "If you compare yourself with others, you may become vain and bitter…" This quote was on a poster on the wall of most of my friends' bedrooms in the 70s. We had no idea what it meant, it just sounded deep and mature. Here I was at 50, finally getting it.

Clean Time, 2012
LEARNING TO FLY

IT IS THE SUMMER OF the Olympics. I am living in a halfway house and I am volunteering at an RSPCA charity shop. I am finding small pockets of joy in other people's old stuff. Sometimes in other people's pockets. An old Eurostar ticket as a bookmark in a textbook on diseases of the gum in the elderly. What poor, misguided periodontist in training decided to use the journey to Paris to read about infected fissures in the upper jaw? A phone number on a bar napkin: "Jorge: the guy with piercing blue eyes at All Bar One. Call Anytime! xxx" This in the back left-hand pocket of a pair of designer jeans. I try the jeans on. They fit beautifully. I think about ringing Jorge, but I have no credit on my phone.

I do shifts of four or five hours, about as much as I can take of going through big black bin liners stuffed with the most random mixture of things: a Spice Girls sticker book, a physics exercise book filled with long diagrams and formulas, and one page in the middle, scrawled in hard angry paper-ripping Biro: FUCK THIS FUCKING BORING SHITE. The discarded detritus, little of it fit for resale, of other people's lives. It is, unknown to me, a litmus test for how I will deal with other people's stuff when cleaning for money. I love it. Every little thing tells a story. Off drugs, everything, initially, is a little bit amazing.

During one shift. a frazzled woman comes in, carrying an injured bird in a towel. She goes, "This is the RSPCA, right?"

I say, yes, it is, but it is the retail bit; we sell stuff to help fund the animal rescues, but we don't actually rescue the animals.

She stares, uncomprehending. She says she has to go to work and will I please deal with the bird. She found it near a tree near her house in such-and-such road off Stoke Newington High Street. Her son was very distraught about it. I open up the towel and the bird is actually standing, but not moving. The woman leaves; we stick the bird in a cage we have in the back and I try to ring the rescue bit of the RSPCA, the real RSPCA.

The real RSPCA advises me to bring the bird to somewhere near where it was found, then wait with it and take observations. The bird will probably revive when it gets to where it was found.

"That is just…beautiful," I sob down the line. "He just wants to go home, and… it's like the Oscar Wilde story about the bird and the statue. No wait, not that one, the bird dies…" Here fresh tears. Everything makes me cry. Everything is so beautiful.

It starts chucking it down and I, as the junior member, am elected to go to the street, find a tree or bush or something not concrete, and release the bird.

So I am walking down the High Street in the horizontal rain, with the caged, stunned bird. We get to the approximate house and I find an approximate tree. I open the door to the cage and the bird squawks and hops out frantically into the road, right in front of a car zipping down it. Just before what seems the inevitable impact, the bird finds its power of flight and soars over the car. I feel ecstatic. I watch it glide gracefully over the row of houses, higher and higher, out of sight.

Chapter Twenty-Six

When I "graduate" from rehab, I get a big file, with all my written work and laminated certificates. I have one for completing the detox and one for completing the rehab. I am wondering how these will look, framed, on some study wall. Does anyone actually display them? My written work reveals a handwriting so shaky at times it turns into a line careening down the page. I have kept a journal. On three of the pages, I have written just, "Help. Need vicar. Need medicine."

I am excited and terrified. I am not yet on speaking terms with the new normal. There is a vast difference between being normal for rehab and normal for real life. In rehab, nobody bats an eyelid if you suddenly drop to the floor or start crying. Oh, they help, but they don't think it's strange. They have detoxed me, made me a little bit nicer, but have not given me the tools, not yet, to be normal and nice when not on drugs. Not that I was either of these things on drugs, far from it. Now I am a blank slate. A blank slate who desperately wants to see her children.

I had travelled down with two broken ribs, a serious dependency on so-called legal drugs, and very little will or curiosity to see what life held in store. I travel back, ribs fully healed, no longer chemically dependent but uncertain where I stand with anyone, if I have any friends left, if I will be able to stick with the programme, with the quivering brethren of substance-dependent misfits meeting in cold halls, mainlining instant coffee and bourbon biscuits, or will retreat back into the hideous small world of corner shop, internet shop, bedsit and dirty doctor.

My good friend Justine meets me at Paddington with flowers and hope. She warns me my bedsit will look very different to me sober and not on drugs from how it did when I was pissed and on lots of drugs. We get back to the room I had called home for a year. The walls are black with damp. My pictures of my children and friends have peeled off in great wallpaper strips, and are lying curled up on the floor. Mould and mushrooms have grown in the corners.

I stick the flowers in some water in the sink and go to the corner shop. I can tell the guy is going to plonk my usual airplane bottles of vodka down, but I hold my hand in a stop gesture. It's just the milk and bread, thank you. The next day I make plans to meet up with my aftercare coordinator and arrange a medical appointment with the service looking after me post-detox. This will be my life for a while. Appointments and classes in a church-affiliated aftercare facility, the very one I will be cleaning in a few years. I take lessons in Bible study and art. My artistic ability is that of an eight-year-old streamed into a low-ability group. I feel like a child and draw like one.

I move from my shitty damp bedsit to a slightly bigger one at three times the price. It is over a kebab shop and infested with vermin. The room next to mine was long ago abandoned and the broken windows were an invitation for pigeons to start nesting there, so I get some strange, bird-related respiratory infection. The mattress, thin and perched on milk crates, is infested with bedbugs. I am bitten all over and I have scabies as well. The nurse at the aftercare centre is the only person I know that I can ask to apply the mite-killing potions to the bits of my body I cannot reach.

If you have not been touched, physically, sexually, humanely, kindly, in a very long time, the touch of a virtual stranger, applying lice-killing formula to the small of your back, is a very moving experience. He is wearing gloves, so he will not get it himself, or get the stuff on his hands. His touch is light and swift. As the stuff seeps into the bits I have scratched too hard, I think, this is all I have to look forward to, in terms of human touch, the application of medical potions by professionally kind nurses in drug addict drop-in centres.

Then, my days take on a little rhythm. I wake up early and go to the church centre and do my classes. I usually have some appointment or other with social services or the council or a GP in the afternoon. This is what early recovery looks like, lurching from one appointment to the next. In the late afternoon, I visit my children in my old family home. They are taller, older. They are wary and weary. I don't know how to be with them. I had forgotten they had grown up. I make mountains of fairy cakes, the kind of activity you do with a bored six-year-old on a rainy day. I make more cakes and biscuits than they can eat. I am trying to look like a mum in an advert. I iron their school clothes. I ask for news of school, friends, their lives. They are rightfully cautious, monosyllabic. Neither affectionate nor nasty, just treating me like the stranger I am. I am playing house, except it is no longer my house. I feel like the visiting housekeeper.

"How was school?"

"Fine."

"Anything interesting happen?"

"No."

"Is everything OK, are you getting on with all your mates?"

"Yeah."

"Do you want a biscuit? I've just made some."

"Yeah. You are always making biscuits."

"Tea?"

"Yeah."

This is parenting at its most reductive. I'm pretty sure this sullen, long-fringed, handsome boy, and his sister, this curly-haired, doe-eyed opinionated firebrand, are biologically mine, but they're not really "of me" at all. They're now more of their father's well-executed, emergency two-in-one parent job. No one asked their permission: should we let the bitch come back, even if it's just to iron shirts and make sugary snacks? The indifference is deafening.

"Do your uniforms need ironing?"

"Huh? Dunno. Whatevs."

There is a difficulty with my friends. My friends, my best friends, feel that now I am clean and sober it is OK to give me what for, and they do. They tell me what a shit I had been when I had been drinking, how they were scared I was going to die, how abusive I was, when I said or did something out of turn, which was most days. This goes on for months, getting together, me being shouted at, and then thinking, what's the fucking point? Eventually I say to one, "Look, every time you see me you tell me how shitty I was. I get it. Either you forgive me or just don't be my friend any more because I can't take it, not now, maybe not ever. I am sorry, but I can't give you my fucked-up years back."

No one tells you this bit, how angry people are with you, especially when you clean up, because they think you can handle it. My kids, at various points, were raging. My husband was, is, diplomatic. In the time I was gone he had got really into organising the house the way he'd always wanted it. Minimalist. No books, no art on the walls, no records, no clutter. He kept a file of recipes and made proper dinners from the BBC food website. He kept the kitchen spotless. He is a far better wife than I ever was. He was, and is, a far better parent.

Christmas was coming fast. We had never made it a deal or an ordeal in our various family flats in the past. Kids opened presents, we opened bottles as early as seemed reasonable, at least to me. Now what? How is this Christmas thing going to work, sober?

At the last minute, newly sober, still shaky, still feeling like a tourist in my own home, I decide to take up an offer of cat- and house-sitting for a friend of mine. I get ill, struck down suddenly and violently by a bug that has been doing the rounds. I set up camp on their voluminous sofa, watching old *Top of the Pops* and crawling to the bathroom as my guts explode. It is a lovely, cosy family house and I feel the presence, the vibe, of a very happy, functional family life. A piano with a piece on the top annotated by the piano teacher. The multitude of books and records and cereals to suit everyone's taste. The Christmas card display, the cards made out to all four of them. I am no longer one of four. I cannot fathom getting a Christmas card made out to just me. That would feel worse than not getting one at all.

On Boxing Day I manage to haul myself off the sofa and go back to the family home. There is forced jollity, the feature of most family celebrations but more evident with the return of the recovering native. My son has got this big speaker for his iPod and, in a gesture of what I mistake as son-to-mother love, he plays a song that always made me happy and got me dancing: "Brimful of Asha". I start to dance in my old front room, unaware that the kids are filming me. They later post me dancing on YouTube, not to the innocent pop song I love, but to some heavy motherfuckin' blingy drugs, whores and guns rap song. I laugh at it with all the fake breeziness I can muster. But I can tell this is more than high jinks. This is their way of telling the world I am a nut job with no filter.

Is this how they would define me? I used to wonder that a lot myself when I cleaned the houses and flats of people who had lots of photos of themselves as children. What were they saying? That childhood was the best part, and it was all downhill from there to the grown-up land of jobs and cleaners and delivered takeaways?

I liked these photos, and studied them. Parents in old-fashioned swimsuits, kids with buckets and spades. A tent or villa in the background. Mum wearing shades and a too-large sunhat, wasp-waisted, elegant, like a movie star. Dad sucking in his fortyish stomach, his hairline not quite receded, maybe holding a fish he had just caught for dinner. The details of these photos were always different, but the kids always looked so happy.

Cleaning, London 2015
THE SHOE COLLECTOR

HE IS A LAWYER, ITALIAN, fine-boned, with a generously sized flat in Clerkenwell that looks as if it was professionally cleaned two seconds ago. He gets straight to the point.

"I have the obsessive-compulsive disorder. I have many instructions that must be followed exactly as I say. Otherwise I suffer from the anxiety."

"We can't have that," I say, sympathetically.

"First, you must remove the shoes and put on these," he says, handing me an unopened pack of hotel slippers.

I do as instructed. The slippers in question are made of a fine mesh; they look like the sort of things visitors to factories wear.

"We start in the kitchen, and for this you use the red bucket and this mop, which you must tie up with an old shirt for the fabric."

"What's wrong with the normal mop head?"

"They get so dirty."

"Well, that's kind of the point. Then you rinse them out… or wash them…"

But he raises a perfectly manicured hand and shakes it silently. "Of course, the difficulty is that the shirt becomes unattached to the mop, but you put it back on, like so," and he shows me how to tie the sleeves to the end of the mop. It is a really nice shirt, Jermyn Street for sure, but with teeny-weeny underarm stains.

The kitchen brief takes a long time. Everything has a method, and everything dirty has to be disposed of in a plastic bag, which must be enclosed in another plastic bag, which will then be deposited by the door. Each room has a different set of disposable gloves, a different mop, a different shirt mop-head, different rags. Every surface has one of those little gel bottles of antibac handwash. He shows me one, his prized possession. "This one I get imported; it kills viruses as well," he says proudly.

The bedroom is just a bed, one bedside table with various medications on it, and stacks and stacks of shoes – at least 50 pairs in boxes. The rest – about another 20 pairs of highly polished designer footwear – have those stretcher things inserted into them. All of the boxes have to be removed and hoovered under and all the boxes have to be dusted with a damp cloth. All the shoes not in boxes have to be moved into the hallway, so the carpet underneath can be hoovered, and put back in the same order. He has drawn a rough sketch to show me which shoes go where. His internal world is an anxious mess, but his shoes are perfect.

The clean is torturous. I can do no right, but he never shouts, just does it again, himself, the right way, talking me through his method as one would talk to an idiot, which is what I am starting to feel I am.

At one point he leaves the flat to get some more special cleaning fluid for the white-tiled floors. While he is gone, I am still in shoe-sorting hell, when I happen upon a tiny framed photograph on the other side of the bed, on a small table. It looks to be a younger version of the man, with what I guess are his mother and father. They are a very good-looking couple. She looks like Sophia Loren. He, the son, the lawyer, is leaping, grinning and shoeless, making a sort of flying jump in the sand. Next to him is a lopsided sandcastle, perilously close to the sea. He is covered in sand. The sheer joy of the photo is heart-breaking. What happened to this happy, sandy, shoeless boy, to turn him into this OCD shoe hoarder, his most prized possession seemingly an antiviral hand gel? I don't care to find out, nor do I think he will tell me. At the end of the clean, it is patently clear to both of us that I am not up to standard.

Chapter Twenty-Seven

There is a job and career fair at the drop-in centre. Be a chef! Be a construction worker! Teach English as a second language. Go for a job interview and we'll give you appropriate clothes to wear through a charity that provides smart interview attire for people with no money.

Who is going to give a job to someone not long out of rehab? How to word it in your CV? Travelling? Expanding the mind? Spiritual growth? I mooch and skulk around the various stalls, trying to decide if I want to teach English as a second language or cook food, or lay bricks, or mend cars. All the models on the posters for said career paths are in their 20s and unfeasibly good-looking for the minimum-wage jobs they seem to do. And all laughing! Put some fries in the deep fat fryer. Not only is it fulfilling but also really, really funny.

The people doing the sign-up at the community college are ever so gentle and persuasive. I am not only getting used to people talking to me as if I had special needs but kind of growing to like it. I say I can't decide if I want to cook or teach English as a foreign language. What I mean is, I don't want to do either. I hate eating, the protracted effects of withdrawal still wreaking havoc on my stomach. I also hate the idea of standing up in front of a group of people but I apply for both courses and take the catering course for the sole reason that it is a shorter bus ride.

The fact that the average age of the other students on my course is sixteen is slightly disconcerting. I want to run away and hide when the mum of one of my son's school friends rocks up to sign her son up for the course. There are two other women my age, one who is functionally illiterate and functionally a great cook but needs to get out of the kitchen and into front of house because her menopausal hot flushes are making cooking unbearable. The other woman works in a shop selling what we used to call "fashions": dreadful pleated skirts, usually lemon-coloured, with matching cardigans and blouses with fussy frilly bits. Seaside and retired people dress shops. She'd done this job for over 40 years and fancied a change. And then there is me, an addict in recovery. We stick together, tremulous, shocked at the behaviour of our younger classmates. They shout over the teacher, play music on their phones, stare into space. I stand, shivering in my white overall and net hat, learning how to stabilise a carrot before slicing it. How did I wind up here? What was I thinking?

Around about Christmas time, the head of the department says that a local restaurant is looking for temp staff to help with the Christmas and New Year rush. He is just mentioning this in passing to one of our tutors but I overhear and see it as an opportunity to escape.

I do a trial, mainly loading glasses into a glass-washing machine and then polishing them, and polishing cutlery. The rest of the restaurant staff are highly excitable, entertaining, borderline bipolar Italians. There is no in-between in their world. Everything is either the greatest thing ever, or the shittiest thing ever. In bad moods, they retreat to the world of regional Italian dialects, with lots of angry hand gestures. In good moods, everything is wonderful, brilliant, is fabulous, yes? "Yes, is fabulous" is the easiest answer, as I stand, sweating, loading a dishwasher with glasses that had held potions I dearly wished I could drink myself.

For reasons entirely unclear to me, except that I show up and do the job, they keep me on. For reasons very clear to me, I start drinking again, because it is there, the booze, and no one, as far as I can tell, knows my history. It is normal to sit in one of the booths, at the end of a shift, and drink leftover wine they cannot sell. I sit there, getting easily pissed on an empty stomach, and listen to the Italians' dreams. None of them are going to stay in the restaurant business. They are going to be pop stars or models or artists. I have no plans, except to get mildly drunk but not so drunk that I am too ill to make it to the next shift. I can see the rest of my life panning out in polished glasses and getting quietly drunk. I will pay my own way and not bother anyone. I have it down to a fine art, getting just pissed enough, but not catatonic. For a while. Actually, not that long.

I still go to recovery meetings. The people at the meetings I start to attend after my relapse laugh knowingly. There is no awful thing that I have done that they have not done, worse, in stereo. They get it. There is nothing so appalling, so selfish, so insane, that at least one, usually several, sometimes all, have not done too.

The fellowship people, to me, both in my early sobriety and in the meetings I start to go to with renewed vigour after my relapse, seem otherworldly – simultaneously undergoing some sort of process but also complete. Those with lots of "clean time", i.e. years off drink and drugs, seem almost angelic. Truly recovered people are in a state of quiet and enduring grace. They are just so happy, and so grateful, to be well, and they have a lightness of being that is magnetic and charming. The insistence anonymity initially puzzles me; this thing that is obviously so very good and healing – why are they not bellowing it from the rooftops? It's just not how it works, and to break ranks, even to say, to write, as I do now, that this programme saves lives, feels almost like a jinx, but it would be equally disingenuous not to mention it at all.

I stay clean and sober for a few months and then one of my friends, who is very sick, comes to visit. He is dying. He drives from Wales to London and he takes me out for a ride. His car is littered with empty nourishment drinks. He pulls over into a side street and looks firmly at me and says, "Don't do that THING you do when people die. Don't do it on my behalf. It pisses people off. It pissed me off. It's not necessary. It's gonna happen, sooner rather than later, and everyone will be waiting for you to go crazy. Don't give them the satisfaction. Plus, if you do, I will HAUNT you. It's OK to be sad, in fact I'd be pissed off if you weren't, but don't be crazy sad. Be sad, then live life. You know the song I want at my funeral. It's by the Whispers: 'And the Beat Goes On'. It just does, and you have to keep living."

He dies, while I am visiting my mother in New York. I stay clean and sober, but I howl. It's my first unmedicated death and it doesn't hurt more or less than the others. I wish I had known this 45 years ago.

I stop working nights and start cleaning full time.

Clean Time

I AM BACK IN THE family home after rehab, though I don't live here any more and I'm not particularly welcome, I feel I should make myself useful. If I do housework, they might just forgive all the crazed drinking and drugging shit, and have me back. It is the one thing I remember how to do: housework. I have trouble making connections, reading signals, having normal conversations, but I can move an iron back and forth, or a Hoover, or a mop. Back and forth, it is the same motion, just with different implements on different surfaces. But even this is fraught with uncertainty. I have forgotten that my son's school trousers are made out of some material that melts under an iron. I have to go buy a new iron, and some new school trousers for him.

I am in the queue at Matalan, in Dalston, and I try to have a conversation with the person in front of me. I say, "These boys grow so quickly, I just got him a pair a month ago, but they don't fit him any more, bless him," but this is not another woman buying a cheap school uniform. It is a Turkish guy buying an art photo of the Eiffel Tower. He smiles politely but moves a few inches away from me, in case I decide to continue the conversation.

I am trying to navigate life, drug-free, by striking up conversations with strangers, with varying degrees of failure.

To the lady who runs the egg stall at Ridley Road Market: "It must take you ages to stack them all up."

No response.

"Do you get hipsters asking if they are free range?"

Nothing.

"OK, I'd like to buy an egg."

"One egg????"

"Lightly poached. Gluten-free toast, please."

She finds this so unfunny she actually turns her back to me and swears.

To someone I used to know from the playground in Clissold Park, someone whose name, and whose kids' names, I've forgotten. I remember the son was a mouth-breather, and the daughter was allergic to everything.

"Hey! Longtime no see. How've ya been?"

She looks at me, a brief glimmer of recognition and then a blank stare. She cannot place me. I might have the wrong woman altogether. "Er, kids are fine. For me, you know, juggle juggle juggle, work, home – you know how it is."

I laugh knowingly, completely without knowing how this works. I find myself laughing *unknowingly* at the slightest provocation. If in doubt, presume the person has said something slightly amusing, something you can relate to, or roll your eyes at, in a simpatico way. "How are…um… Jack and Alex? Alex still got the allergy thing?"

"Simon and Chris are fine. It's OK, I forget other people's children's names all the time. In fact, I am really sorry, I can't remember yours, but I remember your face. You used to sit on the edge of the sandpit, reading."

"Yeah! That was ME!" I am delighted she remembers. *"American Psycho!"*

"Well, you were a little eccentric but…"

"No, I used to read *American Psycho*. Patrick Bateman. The businessman psycho."

But I can see the conversation is drifting into something she finds distasteful, uncomfortable.

These conversations don't go well and usually end with the vague promises of modern life that never actually happen. "We must meet for a proper catch-up. Coffee, or something."

Yes, that would be lovely, whoever you are…

***

My daughter and her boyfriend are sitting at the kitchen table, doing homework. I keep dragging trays of cookies out of the oven. It's not my job any more to monitor pre-dinner sugar intake. They like the cookies, but I will not win her back with double chocolate brownies. You don't actually get brownie points for making brownies to make up for all the time you were a lousy mother on drugs.

The kids go upstairs to study without the distraction of all the sugary and buttery smells. I put on the radio and an old song comes on, one my daughter used to sing along to, I think not really understanding the words at the time. It is Jamelia's "Thank You". She is thanking some boyfriend for beating her up because it made her stronger. The song punches me in the stomach and next thing I know I am sobbing on the kitchen floor. Maybe, just maybe, Kitty can see the song in a new light. That having a terrible mother made her stronger. I go upstairs and knock on her door. "Kitty, it's that song you used to love, the one where he beats her up. Remember you used to sing it into your hairbrush?"

Silence.

"It's on the radio now! If you come down, you can still catch it."

Later, much later, she explains to me that you can listen to any song from any time ever, for free, on the internet. There's much I missed. Much to catch up on.

***

I like to have conversations on buses. People think you are mad, if you start a random conversation. But, once they find out you are not, they are relieved, and might even talk back. It's good practice. If they shift uneasily in their seat, you can just get off the bus, as long as you have nowhere you have to be, at a certain time. I am on the 38 headed to Clapton Pond to visit my old friend and exercise teacher. I have a notion I have much to apologise for as I used to show up to some of her classes more than half-cut. Doing exercise on drugs and drink made everything we did in pursuit of the body beautiful seem patently ridiculous and suggestively sexual. I took the class with three other women, all of whom were married to men called David. The exercises worked, as everyone – except for me – was in pretty good shape. I was by now finding that eating got in the way of my drinking and drugging time, and my flesh had melted away and my curves had disappeared. At various stages, the exercises had us splaying our 100-denier-tight-clad legs into sexually gymnastic positions. These lovely women, and their lovely Davids, enjoying their lovely bodies. Me, I am just on the bus, trying to talk to strangers.

What can I say to my friend and exercise teacher that won't sound too weird? "I am sorry that I thought about you lot having sex with your husbands instead of focusing on my core stability." Why apologise for stuff they would never find out anyway? Better that they think me a lush and drug addict rather than a perverted lush and drug addict.

No. What she doesn't know won't hurt her.

Soon we are sitting in her kitchen, cinnamon smells coming from the oven, her cats basking in the sunshine in her garden. This house is so familiar to me. Christmases and Easters and summer breaks, I have stayed here while she and her family were away. I have far more to apologise for, having clumsily broken things, bled on her mattress, while she was paying me to house-sit and feed the cats.

We sit at the table as I try to explain that my programme of recovery involves making right all the things I messed up while on drugs and, although I have not even started this process yet, I am giving her a heads up that I must make amends to her, to her family. We have to make amends to everyone we have harmed, the living and the dead.

My friend says, "Start with the dead ones. They can't answer back."

***

I am on a bus, an omnibus. Buses for everyone, drunk or sober. Tonight, I have been both. I have had a few drinks, and managed to stop before it all got out of hand. This hardly ever works and it usually gets out of hand very quickly, but tonight, I stopped between the third and fourth drink, knowing full well I should have never taken the first one. I sense I have got off too lightly. According to my recovery programme, I should be in prison, a mental institution, or dead. I have not fully appreciated the gravity of my situation. I don't know why I had three drinks, but I do know why I didn't have a fourth. I wanted to know how to get home. After a fourth drink, not having had a drink in many months, I might not have known where I live, or even who I am.

I have a thirsty headache and a creeping sense of dread and hot shame. But I'm not in prison or dead, just on the 55 to Hackney Central. The bus is hitting every pothole in Hackney and, like everyone else on the top deck, I am bobbing up and down. There is a kid in the seat in front of me. He's black and has a long elegant neck, like my son does. That is the only thing he has in common with my son – a long neck – but to me, it's enough to make a connection. He's got a tag sticking out of his collar, ruining the graceful line of his neck. To get my mind off my relapse, I start to obsess about the tag. If it were my son, I would just tuck the tag back in. Don't do it, Michele, he is not your son. He's a random kid, no, a young man. Don't touch the tag, it's not your shirt, not your kid.

The bus grinds to a red-light halt at the corner of Cambridge Health Road and Hackney Road. Do it now, he'll never know. As everything, everyone, is still for a moment, I bring my hand up to his collar and manage to touch the tag without touching his skin and just about have the tag over the lip of the collar when the bus revs back into action and hurtles us backwards and my hand instinctively grabs the back of his shirt. Lightning quick, he raises his hand over his shoulder and grabs mine, the hand that is grabbing his shirt. He has a nice, firm grip. He turns around, still clutching my hand, and shouts, "Da fuck? What da fuck?"

I move my hand in a little up-and-down shaking gesture. "How'dya do?"

He releases my hand and stares at me. The whole top deck of the bus is staring at me. I smile nervously and say, "I was just uh... I have this son, and he has the same neck, well, no, he's white, but... I uh, oh my stop." It's not nearly my stop but I get up from my seat and make for the stairs, quickly, and he shouts after me, "But are you MENTAL, though?"

"Yes," I bellow back. I stop at an off-licence to get something for the long walk home. Yes, I am mental.

***

I am at Victoria Station, waiting for my first un-sedated date in God knows when. I can't actually remember being on a date, not on anything else, but there is no dating agency specifically for people who used to be sedated but are now not sedated.

On my way here, I felt gigantic waves of nausea and panic. I rattled my handbag because that used to be my thing – rattling my bag to hear the pills bounce about in the brown prescription pill jar. But all I had was Tic Tacs and I knew their rattle, slightly different acoustics to the rattle of Valium in a pill jar. Of course, at the end of my using career it was all blister packs, which didn't rattle at all.

The bloke does not live in London, and is coming from enough of a distance that, even if I am not feeling the connection, I will still feel obligated to hang with him for a few hours until it's time for his return coach.

We are meant to meet outside Accessorize on the top level of the station, except I am waiting at the train station and he is at the coach station up the road. Half an hour, two pairs of 100-denier tights and three lots of hoop earrings later, I feel blissfully stood up. I can just go home and try on my new tights and earrings. My phone, a primitive cheap thing my kids call a burner, a drug dealer phone, so cheap you can throw it in the canal in order that the cops don't get it, starts to ring its strange, tinny salsa music sound.

It is the date, winding his way from the coach station, having clocked my mistake after waiting half an hour at the coach station and unable to find an Accessorize there. We do the modern thing of staying on the phone until we spot each other in real life. And there he is, in a skinny cowboy sort of string tie (good) and with a fast walk (also good, though he may have been running at this point) and a good head of hair. We apologise to each other, sizing each other up I guess in the physical sense, and here is where I fall down, because he is not bad-looking, but he is not my husband. I have not been with a man who I am not married to for a very long time. We can't talk about the kids, or our mutual friends, or our relations, because everything is brand new, except me and my date.

We go to Denmark Street where all the instrument shops are, and look at guitars. We go to Costa and have coffee and chat about this and that, nothing in particular and then he asks an innocent question about the Barclays bike stand. He says, "Are those bikes just for bankers?" and it's a fair enough question if you are not from London or any big city where a bank or other company sponsors hire bikes, but suddenly I just think, no. He's a nice enough chap, but he's not my husband and he doesn't know about hire bikes. Deal breaker. I've made the deal up on the spot. At least the anxiety has ebbed, replaced by a low-level irritation, mainly at myself. He's done nothing wrong. I'm just not ready for this stuff.

Still, I try again. The next one is a science fanatic from Russia. We meet up at a place closer to where I live, so I don't have to travel far if it does not go well. He is small in stature, immediately preoccupied by parking restrictions in my borough. I am not a car person and know nothing about where people can park, or drive, or anything. He smells of car interior, not that I get that close but close enough to catch the slightly stomach-churning smell of a man who spends a lot of time in his car. We find a coffee place, in the lobby of a cinema, which is plan B: if we run out of things to say, we can see a movie.

I had mentioned I quite liked science in the exchange of emails, each of us desperate to find some common ground, some reason to meet up. When he comes back from parking the car, wet, because it is drizzling, he smells like the interior of a wet car. I start to feel ill, unable to explain that I am feeling carsick without actually being in a vehicle. He tells me a bit about his wife, who has gone mad. The story is disjointed and sad and he keeps breaking off and staring into the mid-distance. No, not this one.

What on earth do other people do? I am guessing they go to bars, get loaded and sleep together as soon as possible, to get it out of the way, to get right into that familiar zone, when you know how they like their coffee. I feel whatever it is that normal people do on dates will not come easily to me, if at all.

Chapter Twenty-Eight

Addiction is relapsing and remitting by nature. You can be clean for ages and then one year, two years, ten or 20 years down the line, a little "why not, just the one" goes off in your head and before you know it you are back in the madness, navigating phone calls in private with offshore illegal pharmacies who may or may not deliver the goods after you mate-ishly give them your credit card details. The memory of the sheer tedium of getting drugs, taking drugs, and the lies you have to tell to others, to yourself, to keep the deception going – fades into some nether region of the brain that does not register consequences or catastrophes, or the hazards and hurt you have brought upon those you profess to love.

This time, you reason, unreasonably, it will be different. Slipping into broken, piss-smelling phone boxes where you down two miniatures while looking at badly drawn pictures of busty chicks willing to give you a private massage for enough money to probably support their drug habits, you tell yourself, it is OK, for it is for medicinal purposes. The old auntie at the party, at the sherry. Except I am in a pissoir phone box, downing tiny bottles with stealth. The phone box thing is almost funny. It's where Clark Kent became Superman.

It's where, many times, I have entered sober and emerged drunk, three little bottles staring accusingly at me from the top of the disused phone. I have relapsed at least half a dozen times since first getting clean from everything in Bournemouth, not because the booze, as the climber says of the mountain, "was just there", but because the FEAR was still there, and I just did not have the guts or determination to deal with that. With alarming accuracy I can remember every panic attack I ever had, but I can't remember every single time I got out of it on Valium and vodka, because either I blacked out, or some lesser form of amnesia kicked in. And where once I was happy to see Panic Disorder, Agoraphobia, Generalised Anxiety Disorder and Phobias listed in the big old medical diagnostic books, happier still to see the drugs suggested for treating them, I was, and still am resistant to the disease model of alcoholism or drug addiction. Disease, yes, but disease, as in diabetes, or MS, or ME, not really. There is always, somewhere on the spectrum, at some point, an element of choice. So, no, I didn't ASK to be a drug addict or alcoholic, but each time I relapsed, even with a good support system of fellowships at my disposal, I felt I was choosing the seemingly easier thing, which was the dumber thing.

Sometimes I have it in spades – I understand my programme and new way of living – and I have a working design for the rest of my life to follow. Other times, I lose it, maybe even for one day, and find myself in deep trouble, with my family and friends, the people I love the most. The programme of twelve-step recovery I belong to is my lifeline, having saved my sorry arse so many times that I can't really imagine a life without it.

These days, mainly, I cook in restaurants and cafés. The first job I got like this was at a social enterprise opened by Russell Brand, himself an addict in recovery. The only requirement for the job was that you had to be an addict in active recovery. I didn't even have to lie. How strange it is for me to find out, after doing jobs that required long periods of solitude, of thinking, of pushing mops back and forth, of dealing with the stuff of people but not the actual people, that I have acquired a little gang of regulars, that I can not only endure banter and small talk but actually relish it. How nice it is to be the place where people come to unwind. Global reporter Richard comes in, ordering his eggs and coffee and telling me, after years of frontline war reporting, he cannot watch a horror movie. "I have trouble suspending belief," he says in a matter-of-fact Canadian anchorman voice.

"Wow!" I have trouble suspending disbelief. "Richard, you could lie your arse off, and I would believe you."

Young Ben, who does something in media, comes in for a series of lattes, always planning, always cheerful. He proudly shows us his new puppy. "Babe magnet," I call from the pot of soup I am stirring, before backtracking... "Not that you are not a babe magnet without the dog..."

Gary pootles in, sitting down in his chair, having a cappuccino and quizzing me on general knowledge from a newspaper puzzle page. There is an eccentric but lovely egg lady, who likes her eggs "bluish, just gently stirred, barely heated, just small clumps, to be eaten with a spoon, the "French way", she insists, though she is not French and we have no way of knowing if this is how the French do it. There is beautiful Manon, actually Swiss-French, ordering coffee and slumping beautifully over the table in some work-related despair.

"You are so young and beautiful," I say. "Try not to hit real misery until your 40s, at least."

Jimmy from Scotland sets up his little home-away-from-home office, a model of timekeeping and self-discipline. The food he orders from us is always missing something. Eggs but no yolks. Toast but no butter. Coffee but no caffeine. And yet he seems complete: fit, extremely bright and very handy with the one-liners. Stuff is missing from his food, but nothing is missing from him.

Jozef comes in with his camera. He's been out all day doing street photography, capturing all that is beautiful, particularly the beauty in conventional ugliness, with an unerring eye for detail. He brings me presents. Decorative wooden dice. A pure cashmere cardie. A beautiful drinking cup. I have done nothing to deserve these presents and they come unbidden, with love and generosity. Charlie, Erica and Kristen come in, all American expats, all extremely affable, polite, and sharing a quiet understanding that right now, with what we feel is a lunatic for president, we are lucky to be here.

I chop, dice, slice, simmer, sweat, pull shots of coffee, foam up the milk, wait for toast to pop up, watch the windows steam up cosily when it rains. I feel something approaching true happiness. I have another family. They come and go at their own set mealtimes and coffee breaks, but they are mine, their stories are my stories. Keef and Julie announce their engagement in our caff and I well up. The new mums come in, trying to hide their exhaustion behind too-bright smiles. Their prams are as big as small cars. They order decaf, but I can see they are more thirsty for adult conversation. I know that feeling, that cut-off feeling that you are not quite yet fully back in the land of the grown-ups.

I play an oldies station on the radio because every tenth song or so seems to be by the Jackson Five. Michael, long dead himself from a drug overdose, singing "I want you back, again".

And I am back, back in the land of the living. I am of no use to the dead, nor are they, to me.

I walk to work, talking to the ducks along the canal. At two or three, my boyfriend, who works on the canals, comes in, dusty, dirty, tarry, and we have a break and an espresso in our little caff garden. Most days I talk with my kids, or even hang out with them. This is my greatest pleasure and gratitude in life. Just hanging with my kids.

I don't clean any more. The solitude I once craved so desperately repels me.

Sometimes, staring out of the window on a bus, I pass by one of the flats I have cleaned. I wonder who is living there now, or how much the children have grown, or if the out-of-work guy ever got a job. If the drug dealer got busted. If the guy with the Six Million Dollar Man doll collection ever takes the dolls out of the boxes and plays with them. If the shoe collector with OCD has ever gone back to that beach in Italy, and run barefoot through the hot sand, yelping and laughing as he reaches the shore and sinks his feet into the cold, wet sand. If the son of the dead concert pianist ever sits down at the gleaming black, pristine, never-touched-since-she-died piano, rolls up his sleeves, lights a fag and starts to play, with honky-tonk abandon, Little Richard's "Slippin' and Slidin'".

And sometimes I wonder if there is a girl, starting out in life, trying to earn some extra cash, slipping into a huge, silent, burnt-toast-smelling house in a nice part of the city at 8am. Everyone will have gone to work or school. She will get out the bucket, rags, fluids and duster and mop and put them at the foot of the long staircase. She will climb the stairs, with the intention of doing a top-to-bottom methodical clean. Then she will hitch up her skirt and haul one leg over the bannister, steadying herself with the other foot, until she is poised, backwards, giggling, ready to slide down and feel the cold mahogany rush against her thighs, and she will think anything is possible. Anything.